MW00572307

## About the author

Michael Green was born in Leicester in 1927. He is the author of 26 books and plays. His first, *The Art of Coarse Rugby*, a spoof about the lower depths of the game, was an immediate success, eventually selling a quarter of a million copies. This spawned the bestselling *Art of Coarse...* series devoted to those who weren't very good at various sports and occupations including golf, sailing, acting and house moving. Squire Haggard first appeared in the Peter Simple column in the *Daily Telegraph* in the 1960s. His pursuits were eventually adapted for television in 1990 and ran for two series. Most recently Michael Green has published two volumes of autobiography: *The Boy who Shot Down an Airship* and *Nobody Hurt in Small Earthquake*, both well received. He lives in West London.

*Squire Haggard's Journal*

## Prion Humour Classics

| | |
|---|---|
| *Augustus Carp Esq* | Henry Howarth Bashford |
| *Seven Men and Two Others* | Max Beerbohm |
| *Mapp and Lucia* | E F Benson |
| *How Steeple Sinderby Wanderers Won the FA Cup* | J L Carr |
| *The Diary of a Provincial Lady* * | E M Delafield |
| *The Papers of A J Wentworth, BA* | H F Ellis |
| *Squire Haggard's Journal* | Michael Green |
| *The Diary of a Nobody* | George and Weedon Grossmith |
| *Three Men in a Boat* | Jerome K Jerome |
| *Mrs Caudle's Curtain Lectures* | Douglas Jerrold |
| *Sunshine Sketches of a Little Town* | Stephen Leacock |
| *No Mother To Guide Her* | Anita Loos |
| *The Autobiography of a Cad* | A G Macdonell |
| *The Serial* * | Cyra McFadden |
| *The World of S J Perelman* * | S J Perelman |
| *The Education of Hyman Kaplan* * | Leo Rosten |
| *The Return of Hyman Kaplan* * | Leo Rosten |
| *The Unrest-Cure and other beastly tales* | Saki |
| *The English Gentleman* | Douglas Sutherland |
| *My Life and Hard Times* * | James Thurber |
| *Cannibalism in the Cars* | Mark Twain |

* for copyright reasons these titles are not available in the USA or Canada in the Prion edition.

# *Squire Haggard's Journal*

## MICHAEL GREEN

PRION

This edition first published in 2000 by
Prion Books Limited, Imperial Works,
Perren Street, London NW5 3ED
www.prionbooks.com

A catalogue record for this book is available from the British
Library

ISBN 1-85375-399-8

Jacket design by Vivid
Printed and bound in Great Britain
by Creative Print & Design, Wales

# *Contents*

| | |
|---|---|
| *Introduction* | vii |
| *Editor's Note* | xi |
| 1. Haggard at Home | 1 |
| 2. Roderick and Fanny | 17 |
| 3. An Affair of Honour | 35 |
| 4. Taking the Waters | 51 |
| 5. On the Run | 65 |
| 6. Paris Interlude | 81 |
| 7. Roderick's Disaster | 95 |
| 8. The Return | 109 |
| 9. The Knot is Tied | 125 |

# INTRODUCTION

## by MICHAEL GREEN

Squire Haggard was conceived when I was a young reporter on the *Northampton Chronicle and Echo* in 1943. Our weekly companion paper *The Northampton Mercury and Herald* boasted the oldest complete files in Europe, going back to 1720, and once a week it was my job to descend into the basement where they were kept, and make an extract for the feature '200 Years Ago'. The old files were fascinating and frequently the chief reporter would have to send someone down to dig me out and return me to work. The thing that struck me was how dismal the old news was. It consisted largely of lists of deaths from such outlandish diseases as 'griping of the guts', news of disasters at home and abroad, executions and outbreaks of Plague. But then, in 1743 news was brought regularly from London to Northampton by a man on horseback with a couple of pistols stuffed in his boots as a protection against highwaymen.

The eighteenth century was the great age of the diarist, and I read many of the best-known, from Boswell's various volumes to Parson Woodforde, Fanny Burney, William Hickey and George Hilton, the impecunious and bibulous Westmoreland squire. And of course Pepys, from an earlier age. What struck me was their fascination with food (dinner was usually described in great detail and many of the dishes were rather strange by modern standards). Death and illness were also subject to close scrutiny. There seemed a compulsion to record sexual adventures in high-flown language which contrasted with the sordid realities, such as Boswell's romance with a girl who gave him the pox. And there was an obsession with small sums of money.

Squire Haggard (under another name) first saw the light as a spoof eighteenth-century diary in the North-ampton paper between 1948 and 1950. In the early sixties I was making occasional outside contributions to the Peter Simple column in the *Daily Telegraph* and resurrected him under the new name of Haggard and almost immediately the Squire made his TV debut in the BBC programme *Grub Street*, a dramatisation of fictional characters from Fleet Street columns, such as that of Beachcomber in the *Express*. *Squire Haggard's Journal* appeared in book form in 1975 and fifteen years later Eric Chappell (of *Rising Damp* fame) adapted him for two series by Yorkshire TV, starring Keith Barron and Sam Kelly. Almost simultaneously he returned to the *Daily Telegraph*, this time appearing in his own column, and continued there for several years.

And still the old boy won't lie down, after 50 years receiving new life with this revised version of the original book, in which I have incorporated some new material and excised some of the old. I'm grateful to his fans for keeping the flame alive. Indeed in the late seventies there was a Squire Haggard Society at Cambridge University and I was elected President. It folded rather suddenly, probably as a result of trying to imitate the Squire's unfortunate social habits too closely.

# EDITOR'S NOTE

Squire Haggard wrote his Journal by the method used by many great diarists such as Boswell. That is, he did not necessarily write up each day's events immediately, but made notes and wrote at leisure later. This accounts for the fact that he can describe in detail days when he could not possibly have been able to write his Journal, such as when he was 'on the run'. A pecularity is that Haggard sometimes breaks off the story at midnight, no matter what the state of the narrative, and resumes the incident in the next day's entry.

The spelling has largely been modernized, except for one or two more felicitous archaisms such as 'chirurgeon' for surgeon. Contractions have been left as they were, except where the meaning would have been in doubt.

The Journal was discovered hidden in the Muniment Room of Haggard Hall. Some of the manuscript was indecipherable through mildew, and the stains of wine and candle-grease. In some parts, especially those describing amorous adventures, Haggard had actually salivated all over the Journal while writing, causing the ink to run. This has caused some gaps. Others are caused by the fact that Haggard did not bother to write up his Journal every day; while I, as Editor, have removed some entries in the interests of brevity.

M.G.

# Chapter One
## Haggard at Home

*Sept. 16, 1777*: Rain. Amos Bindweed d. from Putre-faction of the Tripes. Jas. Soaper hanged for stealg. a nail. Recvd. from Thos. Gadgrind the sum of 0£ 0s. 1¹/₄d., the farthg. being bad. Shot unusually large poacher in a.m. In p.m. recvd. a bill for 13£ 5s. 6¹/₂d. in respect of some pigs bt. off Jeremiah Rhubarb, which all had the swine fever, so I did not pay him.

Because of the wet weather my Rheumaticks are so bad I was unable to have my usual whore yesterday. As she insists on payment in advance my servant Grunge had her instead, rather than waste threepence. This distressed me not a little as it was my favourite, Perverted Polly of Lower Sodmire.

For dinner ate a rook pie and some pigs' cheek, together with a pease puddg. My portion of the puddg. appeared to be bad so I gave what remained to my wife Tib and was forced to expunge the taste with a quart of claret. ITEM: To purgatives, 0£ 0s. 0¹/₂d.

*Sept. 17*: Hail. Thos. Hogwash garrotted by footpads. Jas. Soaper found to be innocent. My wife Tib turned green in the night and was confined to bed in a.m. Grunge apologised for the pease puddg. He says it

1

should not have been served as it was some they kept for cleang. the silver.

Percvg. a low fellow skulking near the Hall in a.m. I demanded his business and he replied, 'Affairs of the Law' and handed me some writs for debt, among which was one from my Physickan, Dr. Bone, claimg. half a guinea for attendg. the birth of my son Roderick, now twenty-one. I kicked the miserable creature into the lake and sent him on his way with a charge from my fowlg.-piece. I then amused myself by pinng. the writs to a tree and expectoratg. upon them.

To town in p.m. to discuss matters with my Lawyer, whereupon the followg. dialogue ensued, viz:

Self: It is time to set my affairs in order. I am so beset with debt I do not know which way to turn.

Lawyer: You owe me 3£ 4s. 3$^1$/$_2$d. for makg. a new will in the old King's time and that was nigh twenty years ago.

Self: Is that all you have to say?

Lawyer: You must spend less.

Self: Shall I mortgage the Hall?

Lawyer: It is mortgaged already. You tried to mortgage it twice.

Self: D— you, what shall I do?

Lawyer: Shut the door as you go out and pay my clerk 0£ 6s. 8d.

At this I d—d him for a cantg. Attorney and poured a bott. of ink over his head. Departed and kicked an elderly Quaker in the street to relieve my feelgs.

On return to the Hall, called Grunge and the housekeeper, Mrs. Runcible, and informed them their wages would be delayed due to the poor state of my affairs. At this they broke into loud mirth not havg. been paid this year in any case. I then sat down to list my assets and debts by the Double Entry system and this resulted in the conclusion that debts exceeded assets by 995£ 1s. 3¹/₂d.

When I had finished, the sight of all these debts stretched out like a whore in bed overwhelmed me so much I was forced to consume a small pail of claret to restore myself, which I did so satisfactorily that when I came to add the figures up again I appeared to have a surplus of sevl. thousand pounds. But further calcu-lation confirmed my state was hopeless and I was obliged to restore some Animation with a bottle of port. This so invigorated the Vital Powers that I asked Grunge to send me up a girl from the village. But he returned sayg. none would come as they had not been paid for sevl. weeks and then only less than they can obtain from the soldiers, except the Militia, who only pay twopence.

*Sept. 20*: Fog. Wm. Woodbine d. from The Noxious Effluents. Thos. Hogwash buried. Jas. Soaper dug up and removed to Consecrated Ground. Evicted Lame Bob in a.m. recvg. a blow from his stick which well-nigh deprived me of what is left of my manhood. ITEM: Repairing breeches 0£ 0s. 3¹/₂d. Recvd. bill from Lawyer for a penny for ink which I poured over him.

The Rector approached the Hall in a.m. but thinking he had come snivellg. again about my attempt to enclose his Glebe I fired a duck gun over his head and had the satisfaction of seeg. him jump sevl. feet in the air. Notwithstandg. he gained the porch and shouted that tomorrow I was to distribute the Haggard Dole to those villagers who are eligible and in default I was liable to be fined a shillg. a day until it was handed out.

*Editor's Note: The Haggard Dole was a very ancient charity, commuted in the 19th century. It was founded by Sir Tirwit Haggard in 1208, ostensibly as a thanksgivg. for a safe return from the Crusades, but accordg. to local tradition to mark his being cured of a particularly virulent form of pox which he had contracted in Palestine. By its terms a shillg. and a farthg. were to be distributed to all 'worthy women' of the village. The Rector was correct about the fine for non-payment, which would have been levied by the Consistory Court.*

Soon after the Rector left there was a loud noise from the Park and a Gothick Ruin, erected by Capability Brown a few years ago, collapsed. Fortunately, he is still owed 1,000 gns. Dined at an inn upon a mutton puddg., but the inside of this being bad I was constrained to eat round the edge. I called the landlord and rammed his face in the remainder, d—ing him for a d—d cheatg. dog, to which he made no reply, his face being in the puddg.

*Sept. 21*: At five o'clock the women gathered in the churchyard for distribution of the Dole, the shillg. and a farthg. which every woman in the parish (exceptg. Prudence Peascod, who is a witch), receives from my hand. Prudence Peascod endeavoured to attend in disguise but was recognised by her pointed ears and ducked in the pond. One female present was not known to me, a wench called Betty Bouncer, lately come to the village. The sight of her delicious white bubbies so excited my Amorous Propensities that I pressed her hand as I gave her the money and asked if she would like a *greater gift* than a mere shillg., viz: the opportunity to become a Lady of Quality.

She replied, 'To achieve such a prize I would do anything Your Lordship might require,' so I whispered in her ear to come to my room at 10.30 that eveng. when she would receive *her prize*.

The thought of enjoyg. the girl's favours threw me into such agitation that I was hardly able to hold a quart of Madeira to my lips at supper, after which I immediately retired to my chamber to await my entry into the Tournament of Love. I had given instructions for the girl to be admitted instantly, and at 10.30 there was a knock on the door and a figure entered in hood and cloak. Seeg. my beautiful prize within my grasp I was seized with such Amorous Fervour that I begged her to delay not an instant but to throw off her garments and conjoin with me immediately.

'I will not forget my promise to make you a Lady of Quality,' I cried. 'You shall be my wife in all but name and shall have sixpence as well for being a good girl tonight!'

At this the figure threw back her hood to reveal the features of my wife. Seizg. a warmg.-pan she began to screech and belabour me with such vigour that I was forced to flee from the room in my nightshirt and take refuge in the outside privy, where I spent the night. ITEM: To repairg. Gothick Ruin 1£ 2s. 6¹/₂d. ITEM: To repairg. door of privy, 0£ 0s. 11³/₄d.

N.B. The wench did not arrive in any case.

*Sept. 22*: Jem Hornpipe drowned when he fell into

5

the brook; he would have lived but being drunk he fell asleep and was carried away. They found only his hat.

*Sept. 23*: Gales. The Coroner has sat upon Jem Hornpipe's hat and declared it was not enough to return a verdict on; Jas. Soaper dug up by anatomists. This was feared, as his ears were of different sizes, which much interested sevl. doctors.

*Sept. 24*: Rain. No mortalities published today as the Parish Clerk himself died from divers diseases, the least of which were The Green Emissions and A General Constriction of the Pipes, although some say he was poisoned by Blind Billy, whom he caused to be put into the stocks for poking him in the eye with his stick.

Observed Crippled John near Long Bottom in a.m. and knowing he was searching for conies I shot away his crutch with my fowling-piece, and was much amused at his efforts to escape, which he did with astonishing celerity. While pursuing him I discovered an amazing sight, viz: five score gypsies and tinkers were encamped in Long Bottom. I demanded what they wanted and they answered insolently that they had come to make festival and it was none of my business.

'This will teach you whose business it is!' I cried and raised my weapon, but a fellow seized the barrel and snatched it from me, so I was forced to flee, being peppered in the back by my own bullets, which I made Grunge dig out in the evening for further use.

*Sept. 25*: Wind. Tertius Hogbinder hanged. Saw the Constable in a.m. about the gypsies but he says he can do nothing; I must seek an injunction at law. Ate some oxbrains and chaps at dinner with tatties; drank three botts. of Madeira and one of Canary. Lacking amusement I asked Grunge to stand still while I threw fruit at him.

'If you use me so barbarously,' be said, 'I shall not tell you how to get rid of the gypsies.'

'Do that' I cried, 'and you shall name your own price!'

*Sept. 27*: Hail. Parish Clerk buried. Blind Billy danced around making vulgar signs as the coffin was lowered. He then unbuttoned his breeches and made water into the grave with unerring accuracy despite his infirmity; he is now in the stocks again.

Afterwards, to Long Bottom to see Grunge's Stratagem. I observed him to wander into the camp with a cowl over his head like a beggar. Then he drew back the cowl to reveal a face covered in red spots and began to howl, 'Will no one take pity on me?'

They asked if he was ill. 'Aye,' he replied. 'I have spots all over my body and a swelling in the armpit and fear it is the Tokens of the Plague, for this field is notorious for pestilential vapours which arise from the soil. But they do say the remedy is to lick a gypsy's face, which is why I am come among you good people that I might lick somebody's face and be cured.'

With which he stuck out his tongue to a great length and leaped upon the gypsies, who fled with cries of, 'The Plague! He has the Tokens! Let him not lick you!' And soon every single one had run away, leaving the field deserted except for Grunge cleaning his face with a handkerchief.

'Well done, Grunge!' I ejaculated, 'you have saved the Hall from despoilation by those vagabonds. I said name your own price, but I shall give you what is beyond price, and that is the gratitude of an English gentleman. And, should you wish more, you shall have an extra piece of coal for your fire this very night.'

He gave no thanks for my generosity but instead replied, 'That is funny, but these spots will not come off. Could it really be the Plague? Oh sir, let me lick your face and cure myself.' He then flung himself at me and I was forced to climb a tree to escape. Nor could I get rid of him except by throwing down a guinea so he could see a doctor. The rogue took it and went away shouting, 'I feel better already.'

*Sept. 28*: Rain. Wm. Turnover d. from the Emetick Spasms. An unusual occurence happened as I passed down the High St. this morning, viz: as I passed the shop of Mr. Spoke, the wheelwright and coachbuilder, I percvd. him standg. outside the premises in the doorway. Since I owe him 0£ 0s. 1½d. for repairs to my chaise three years ago I greeted him cordially but he made no reply.

This lack of civility from one whom Providence had ordained should serve others vexed me considerably and poking him with my stick I animadverted as follows, viz: 'Sir, when a gentln. takes the trouble to bid you good day, you might at least have the civility to acknowledge it. Instead you are merely standg. there, sticking your tongue out at me.'

I then realised the miserable mechanick was not standg. but hanging from the end of a rope attached to the bracket of the sign over the shop. Help was summoned and the wretched individual cut down, after which he revived and confessed he had tried to do away with himself because of the fall in trade occasioned by the Agricultural Depression, which has meant the gentry are purchasing no new carriages.

Thus are we all ruined by the fall in Commerce; my own debts weigh heavily upon me. My spirits were so depressed that I inadvertently put a penny in Blind Billy's hand as he stood begging. I tried to take it back but his fingers had closed on it with immense strength.

*Sept. 29*: Hail. Jas. Weevil whipped at the tail of the hangman's cart for statg. that The Archbishop of York was an old Sodomite. The Coroner has sat on Wm. Turnover but fell asleep before he could return a verdict. Charity Barker died from the Mange.

Ate a dish of lung with some chitterlings and a plum puddg. for dinner; also a pie but I know not what was in it except it had a beak. Grunge came to me after the meal, behavg. v. strangely, tip-toeing into the room and whispering and tapping his nose. I implored him to speak up and he hissed furtively in my ear that Mr. Moonshine was outside.

'Mr. Moonshine, the smuggler!' I ejaculated. 'I must see him at once.' I went instantly to the front door where a man stood shrouded in a cloak. 'On the cart behind me, sir,' he said, 'is a small barrel of French brandy which fell off the stern of a schooner in Lyme Bay. You may have the same cheap.' Within seconds the transaction was complete and I hastened inside rolling my treasure before me and gloating over the delights to come.

*Sept. 30*: Drizzle. Grunge, who at times has a Philosophick turn, does not approve of my smuggled brandy barrel.

'One day, sir,' he said, 'there will be no barriers to trade and the smugglers will be out of business. I foresee a time, perhaps in about 223 years, when all Europe will be one; when trade will pass unhindered between all States without the imposition of excise and men will sail to Calais and return laden with as much French wine as they can carry. Yet no Revenue Officer will hinder them.'

At this my face grew stern and I spake harshly. 'Let me never hear such sentiments again in this house!' I cried. 'Mark my words, the day this country allies itself to those mincing pederasts, papists and dancing-masters in Europe will see the end of all we value. Our golden sovereigns will be replaced by *groschen* or *livres*; our roast beef supplanted by fricassees; our lives subject to the whim of envious French officials. I would pay double, aye treble, for brandy rather than see that happen.'

Decided to sample my brandy at dinner. I was just pouring myself a glass when Grunge rushed into the room exhibitg. tokens of the deepest agitation. 'Sir,' he cried, 'we are lost! The Excise men have arrested Mr. Moonshine and are approaching the house in search of smuggled brandy. They will be here in half-an-hour. There is no escape – they will search everywhere. We must pour it into the pond.'

'Pour it away?' I cried. 'Never shall it be said a Haggard poured away a drop of such precious fluid. There is only thing to be done and that is for us to drink the barrel before they arrive.'

So we set to with a will and I know not what the Excise men said as it was two days before I regained my wits and Grunge lay insensible for 24 hours. ITEM: The

Curative Powders, 0£, 0s. 0¹/₂d.

*Oct. 2*: Rain. Elijah Doghouse d. from the Manifold Eruptions. Awoke late and immediately rang for Grunge but there was a terrible wailg. from the corridor and he burst into the room shouting and sobbing as if distracted with grief.

'What's the matter?' I cried and he replied: 'Matter enough! The worst news since they raised the tax on gin. Slavering Sally, the favourite whore at Lower Sodmire, has died from exhaustion as a result of plying her trade too freely at the Yeomanry Ball!'

On receipt of these Dread Tidings a paroxysm of distress smote me and for a moment I could not articulate. At length I ejaculated, 'What happened?' and Grunge, between sobs, told me that when Perverted Polly, another whore at Lower Sodmire, was stricken with a fever, Sally generously offered to oblige her customers as well as her own.

Alas, the effort proved too much and she succumbed peacefully, blessg. all her clients and returning any money taken in advance. 'She died like a true Christian,' declared Grunge, 'in the service of others,' to which I cried, 'Amen!'

*Oct. 3*: Fog. Feeble Frederick d. from a surfeit of apple puddg. His wife threw it at him, killg. him instantly. The dreadful news about Sally has struck me to the heart. Many the time I have sent for her when life was unbearable.

I wept as I remembered her habit of bitg. each penny she recvd. to make sure it was good. She had other habits too, which I shall not set down. She had no faults except a tendency to smear her armpits with garlic against the Plague.

When the first paroxysm of grief was over I determined she should have a fitting memorial and prepared the followg. funeral tribute, viz:

ELEGY ON THE DEATH OF A WHORE WHO DIED DOING HER DUTY

Ye gods of Love! ye gods of War! look down
On one whom Love has cruelly o'erthrown.
Have mercy on this simple little whore
Who fell a soldier in the Paphian's War.

She died the noblest death that one could will
Serving mankind with all her subtle skill.
The warriors of Mars with her made free,
Number Five Troop, the Loamshire Yeomanry.

Alas, her favours were too freely given!
Her mortal frame succumbed, by Cupid riven.
Yet even dying spake she gen'rously:
'I'm sorry, lads, but I'll return your fee.'

For little Sal, ring out no mournful chimes,
She lives elsewhere in heaven's happier climes!
Where clients pay their money on the nail
And pox and clap are but a fairy tale.

When the poem was finished I shed a tear on the page and carried it to the Rector to read it at her funeral but the cantg. hypocrite declined and said it was blasphemous and I would do better to fall to my prayers. 'Then I shall read it myself at her obsequies,' I shouted.

*Oct.* 5: Took my Elegy to the funeral of Sally; a huge crowd of three thousand souls, all men, attended, exhibiting tokens of the deepest sorrow. Many appeared to be in the last stages of disease but gallantly limped behind the cortege or were carried on litters, moang. and beatg. their breasts. The Band of The Yeomanry played mournful airs.

The only discordant note was struck by sevl. wives who tried to spit upon the bier. As the coffin was lowered I cried, 'Silence!' and started to read aloud the poem. Alas, after the first verse I slipped on the wet earth and fell into the grave. The gravediggers, however, were tenants of mine and the dogs pretended they did not see me. So they lustily filled in the trench and I was half-buried before I could clamber out. ITEM: Clean raiment, 0£ 0s. 4$^1/2$d.

N.B. I shall send my ode to *The Gentleman's Magazine*.

*Oct.* 6: Jas. Hosepipe d. from The Stone. It fell off a high wall and hit him on the head. Plague raging in Constantinople. Signs of the Stagnation in Commerce everywhere. *The Intelligencer* says the popping of champagne corks in 'Change Alley has been replaced by the banging of pistols as stockjobbers shoot themselves or are shot by their clients. How thankful I am that my own money is invested safely in a company for Buildg. A Tunnel Under the Irish Sea.

*Oct.* 7: Eli Bilgewater d. from The Gravel. This a.m. shot a most interestg. poacher, one of the most unusual I have ever fired upon. A great, black-bearded fellow, he seemed impervious to my first charge of birdshot and led me a merry dance up hill and down dale before I finally cornered him in Long Meadow.

I was so pleased with the chase I told him I would pay him a shillg. if he would offer himself as a target again, there being a dearth of hares and rabbits this year. He said I was a fine old English gentln. and it would be a pleasure to be shot by me but he regretted business called him elsewhere. With which he fled.

*Oct. 8*: Gales. The sexton got drunk and fell into a newly-dug grave today. As he lay insensible, he was stolen by two body-snatchers and sold to an anatomist.

In a.m. called servants together and told them we must economise due to the Depression in Trade, which has caused rents to dwindle to almost nothg. 'No more of those expensive dishes,' I cried. 'Simple, cheap fare is the rule from now on. I shall set an example by not havg. a whore this week.'

At dinner Grunge brought in a strange dish which gave off a revoltg. smell. 'What is it?' I ejaculated, and he replied, 'It is a stew made from the intestines and bladder of a sheep, sir. Very cheap and nourishg. I obtained the ingredients *gratis* from the slaughterhouse where they give them away to the poor.'

He then poured a strange, colourless liquid into my glass and when I animadverted, 'Is it not a little early for spirits?' he said, 'It is water, sir.'

*Oct. 9*: Slept ill due to my dinner. Awoke from a nightmare to find Grunge standg. by the bed holdg. a newspaper.

I asked what he wanted and he replied, 'Sir, you are a

ruined man. The price of stocks has collapsed.'

'I know, you fool,' I cried. 'I suppose you are going to say my ten million South Sea shares are worthless? I knew that well enough.'

'No sir,' he said. 'It is your 20,000 shares in a Company for Building a Tunnel Under the Irish Sea. they are now worth only three halfpence.' 'Each?' I asked and he said, 'No, altogether.'

I asked Grunge what I should do and he said it was customary under these circumstances for a gentln. to take his own life. He had assisted sevl. former employers to hang themselves and he would be happy to assist me; indeed, he had a special rope in his room which he kept for such melancholy occasions or if preferred a silver pistol, suitable for use by the gentry.

However, I told him I preferred to drink myself to death and intended to start immediately, therefore let him bring in the port, with which I set to with a will and damnation to all the rogues on 'Change.


*Oct. 10*: Hail. Ebenezer Cartwheel d. from the Windy Convulsions. Bart. Wheeler hanged. His last words were, 'May you all rot.' There is much talk of the homeless mendicants which plague the land. In London some of them have taken to sewing loops of cloth in the backs of their coats. They then hang themselves up on the spikes of the railings in front of houses and sleep vertically.

Sevl. large houses in Pall Mall have been affected. Lord Chesterfield, on returng. home in the early hours recently, found half-a-dozen nomads hanging on his railings and played a tune on their heads with his stick. He reported the men's skulls gave off a bass note while the women and children had a higher tone.

*Oct. 11*: Rain. Fredk. Seedcake hanged for stealing a lamb. His last words were, 'Glug'.

In a.m. was much disturbed to see some mendicants occupyg. a grave in the churchyard. The Rector says that when he rang the bells this morning five dropped out of the belfry.

*Oct. 13*: Thunderstorms. Prudence Barnwell died from Gout in the Spleen.

Passing through the Park in a.m. I saw an old man sheltering under a tree, drenched by the storm. I approached and after hitting him over the head with the cudgel I use on poachers said, 'Away, idle Whig-voting homeless mendicant and seek work or I shall set the dogs upon you!'

He looked me in the eye and replied thus, viz: 'So, Haggard, you do not recognise the starving man who stole a shilling from you at the Fair twenty years ago. I went to London and made my fortune but never forgot the crime; I swore on The Good Book to repay you ten thousandfold. Today I came to keep my oath and give you 500£.'

With a cry of dismay I fell on my knees and began brushing water from his breeches but he went on: 'And this is the welcome I receive! No money shall you have, vile Haggard, it shall all be given to the homeless people, who suffer as I once did.'

With which he turned and strode away to town where shortly afterwards I heard the merry shouts of mendicants as he distributed his fortune.

# Chapter Two
## Roderick and Fanny

*Oct. 14*: Mist. Virtue Goodbody died from the Putrid Exhalations. This being the shooting season I invited a party to be my guests for a few days' sport, hoping some of them might lend me money. At dawn we repaired to Ghoul's Field and waited for Mellors, my gamekeeper, to send over the birds. But nothing happened for some time and then a solitary pheasant rose before us and observing the guns pointing at it sank back to the ground.

I asked Mellors what the D— was happening. He said it had been a bad year, what with the lack of rain and the poor harvest and the fact I hadn't paid his wages and he had raised only a few birds and most of them were too weak to fly.

I apologised deeply to my guests for this unfortunate lack of sport but a young Corinthian, The Hon. Fortescue Molehurst, suggested we could shoot the birds and have them for supper.

'Shoot a sitting bird!' I ejaculated. 'Only a French-man would do such a thing. No, we will save powder and shot and hit them on the head.' But this proved easier said than done as the birds showed unusual agility considering their sickness and the attempt was

17

abandoned after somebody smote Sir Jas. Card on the foot with the butt of their fowling-piece, causing him to swoon with pain.

*Oct. 15*: Rain. Jeremiah Barnwood died from the Black Eruptions. Still no pheasants so in a.m. the party went out and shot anything in sight, returning with a bag of three crows, one wood-pigeon, a rat and Blind Billy, who strayed across the line of fire and received some pellets in his back. With shooting curtailed in p.m. we were forced to amuse ourselves by holding an Expectoration Contest as to whom could spit the best, using Grunge as a target. This was won by the Hon. Fortescue Molehurst who struck Grunge on the cheek from a distance of nineteen paces to thunderous applause. I thanked Grunge for his pains but he said it was an honour to be spat upon by a gentln.

The guests will return home disappointed unless Mellors can do something and I fear they will be angry with me. I called upon Mellors but he said matters were no better and I therefore had to resort to a Stratagem.

*Oct. 16*: Gales. Arose early and the guests took up positions near Ghoul's Field while a whistle was blown for the signal to start. For a moment there was silence and then a loud rustling was heard in the undergrowth and a vast feathered creature, full six feet high and waving its wings desperately ran across the line of fire.

It was Mellors, whom I had commanded to dress in feathers and provide some sport for the guests. For a moment they were stunned and then with loud cries of exultation emptied their barrels at the creature which dodged this way and that, emitting shrieks of pain and fear, before it jumped over a hedge and was seen no more.

Thus my guests went home happy declaring it was the best day's shooting they had ever had and Mellors escaped with nothing worse than a few pellets in him, in recompense of which I gave him a handsome present. ITEM: To Handsome Present for Mellors, 0£ 0s. 1½d.

*Oct. 17*: Gales. Mortalities: Stoppage of the Blood, 3; Reticulation of the Loins, 28. *The Intelligencer* reports a speech by one Thos. Paine, who promised that soon Jack wd. be as good as his master, every man would have five acres and a cow and there would be pensions and schooling for all from the Publick Purse.

*Oct. 19*: Hail. Nathaniel Blastoff d. from Excessive Fornication. This a.m. Grunge asked to borrow *The Intelligencer*. Shortly afterwards I rang the bell and asked for another bottle of Madeira as I had dropped one on the floor and was too drunk to pick it up.

'Perhaps, sir,' he replied.

I demanded to know what the D— he meant by 'perhaps, sir' and he said the speech reported in *The Intelligencer* had affected him greatly. I told him I would affect him greatly if he paid attention to such nonsense but he answered, 'Man is born free but is everywhere in chains.'

The Madeira never came and when I rang for more coals the maid told me Mr. Grunge said, 'Would I mind putting them on myself as he was engaged in readg. the works of Jean-Jacques Rousseau.'

I sent the girl to the village with a message for

Common Kate, the whore, to come as usual but she returned with a note from Kate saying Mr. Grunge had advised her not to come unless I paid a penny extra and gave her a paid vacation at Christmas. I turned to drink but Grunge refused to bring anything from the cellar. 'Then you are dismissed!' I shouted but he merely replied, 'Thank you sir, I have not been paid for four years in any case.'

*Oct. 24*: Rain. Grunge has been spreading his evil philosophy all week with the result the labourers say they will not work more than fifteen hours a day and even little Nellie Nobody, the scullerymaid, refuses to satisfy my wants just for a new ribbon but demands an orange as well.

In p.m. I therefore addressed Grunge. 'I have been deeply impressed by your new-found convictions,' I said, 'and have decided to yield to your views. I wish to make you a present of the estate.'

His bovine face glowed and I went on, 'Unfortunately, the estate is mortgaged heavily. There are debts and unpaid taxes of 1,000£, I expect a writ any day and in default I shall go to the County Gaol. All this is now yours.'

He gave a wail and fell to his knees. 'Please, sir,' he cried, 'Do not let me go to gaol. I will do anything.'

'Good,' I replied, 'then bring in dinner for a start. And stand near in case I wish to kick you,' with which he scurried away and I settled back to enjoy myself with the Old Order restored.

*Oct. 31*: Rain. Obadiah Pumphouse thought he saw the Devil crossing Five-acre Meadow and went mad.

Ebenezer Loudmouth d. from A Seizure of the Pipes. While I was eating some cow's foot and a boiled tongue for dinner in p.m. a strange incident occured, viz: a hideous face, glowing with fire, appeared at the window and there was the sound of unearthly laughter.

At first I feared it was due to drinking too much Madeira but as I had only consumed a small vat I knew this could not be the cause and I trembled lest it was the ghost of somebody I had evicted. Then I realised the face was a hollowed-out turnip with a candle inside and as this was the Eve of Hallowmas, I was the victim of a prank.

Soon afterwards another ghastly apparition appeared at the window but this time I was ready for it. I seized the special club I keep for poachers, flung open the window and smote the apparition on the head. But even as my club was about to fall I realised with dismay that the apparition was not a vegetable but Distorted Daniel, whose face is twisted into a dreadful smile owing to Apoplexy and who had doubtless come to beg me not to distrain upon his old mother. The club descended with terrible force and the face vanished with a fearful cry.

*Nov. 3*: Fog. For three days I have lived in mortal fear of arrest for the murder of Distorted Daniel. We cannot find his body and he must have dragged himself off to die. I asked Grunge whether Distorted Daniel counted as a human being, since he has no wits, but Grunge replied I would be hanged even if he had been a sheep or a Roman Catholic.

As I sat drinking myself into insensibility in p.m. a strange event occured, viz: there was a ghostly knocking on the window. I fell to my knees in terror crying, 'I did not kill him, it was Grunge I tell you,' when the window opened and a total stranger climbed into the room.

'Do you not recognise me?' he cried. 'I am Distorted Daniel. The shock occasioned by the blow on my head restored my visage. My mouth is no longer twisted right round. I can speak without deafening myself and eat without stuffing food into my ear. In short I am whole again and owe it all to you.'

With which he fell on his knees crying, 'Bless you, sir, for a fine old English gentln.' Thus out of evil came good and I determined to reform, in celebration of which I drank five botts. of port and kicked Grunge upstairs.

*Dec. 5*: Rain. Ebenezer Rathole d. from the Windy Spasms. A gypsy woman called upon Theodore Mainbrace and tried to sell him some pegs, at which he swore at her for an idle rogue, whereupon she placed a curse upon him as a result of which he is said to have been turned into a stoat. This is known to be true because he has vanished and a stoat now sits in his place at the table. It enjoys the same food as the former master of the house and after dinner goes to sleep in his chair. When a Priest passed by in the street it leaped to the window and hissed at him.

Ate a sheep's head with Roots and some eels for dinner. Am not sure if all the eels were quite dead, but no matter. My spirits are so low what with the debts that beset me and the Depression in Trade and Agriculture that trifling matters are of no import. My wife Tib is gone to her sister, yet her absence failed to cheer me.

However, spirits were raised in p.m. when hearg. a

great halloo-ing outside I went to the door to find my son Roderick had arrived home from Oxford University, bringing with him a college friend called Willikins who was so drunk he was strapped to the roof of the coach. Alas, my cellar is reduced and I could scarce find a dozen botts. of claret for us to drink at supper.

*Editor's Note: Although Roderick was Squire Haggard's only legitimate son, he had several natural sons and daughters by village girls and others and they sometimes took upon themselves the name Haggard.*

*Dec. 6*: Drizzle. Mortalities: Dry Serpigo, 2; the Blains, 3; Imposthume, 1; Lethargy, 5.

Despite my poverty treated Roderick and Willikins to a special dinner, viz: cods' heads, salt beef, pigs' feet, rook pie, some lung and a plum puddg., with a couple of gallons of claret. Roderick complained the rooks were full of old nails and begged me to use proper bullets next time.

Thinking that now Roderick was a man of learning he and his friend might like some intellectual conversation, invited the Rector to meet them; I hoped Roderick and the Rector would exchange Latin Jests, but when the Rector quoted 'Bis dat qui cito dat,' Roderick merely replied, 'And the same to you, sir' and started telling how he had been cheated by a girl on Christchurch Meadows.

He then asked the Rector if he knew anything about boxing; on receiving a negative he gave a detailed account of a prize-fight at Oxford in which the spectators were covered in blood which spouted from the contestants; at this point the Rector fainted and Willikins vomited over him, so the visit was not a success.

After dinner Roderick asked me to pay a college debt he had contracted for wine last term.

'Pay your College debts?' I cried. 'I could as well pay the National Debt, I am so short of money. I tell you I have not even had a whore these three days.'

To this he replied, 'Tush Father, why are you worryg.? By the New Year you shall be as rich as a London Alderman, for I have come home to tell you the news that I am affianced to a Lady with 10,000£ in the Funds in her own right, and 500£ a year beside, and a dotg. Father who will give her away with a fortune!'

This joyous announcement brought such a great feelg. of bliss that I immediately consumed a pint of Madeira. As I was doing so, Roderick explained that his Beloved's name was Fanny Foulacre, and she is the only daughter of Sir Josh. Foulacre, of Foulacre Hall, not forty miles from here. He met Miss Foulacre at a ball in Oxford, where she frequently goes to visit her Aunt. She was obviously smitten by Cupid's Darts; he pressed his suit with the connivance of the Aunt; and they are now secretly affianced. In the New Year we are invited to Foulacre Hall, where Roderick will formally ask for her hand and her fortune.

'And I have good reason to know I shall have it,' he declared, 'for that old b—h of an Aunt of hers had told me Sir Josh. despaired of ever getting Fanny off his hands and regards this chance as sent from Heaven.'

The glad news brought us great merriment and we toasted Fanny Foulacre, and a speedy death to her rich father, and long life and prosperity to us all with a three times three, and Willikins danced a quadrille on the spinnet. ITEM: To spinnet, 1£ 10s. 0½d.

*Dec. 7*: Barnaby Toadstool attempted to drown himself, but was rescued by Half-Witted Jack, whom he knocked unconscious for his pains. Plague raging in Florence. Bt. off Fredk. Hayseed one plough, but it turned out to be useless as the ploughshare is bent and it will only go round in circles. ITEM: To bent plough 0£ 0s. 11¾d.

Roderick informed me in p.m. it is his intention to settle all family debts as soon as he is married, after which he will run into fresh debt on the strength of his father-in-law's purse. I heartily approved of this excellent scheme of Domestick Economy. Whilst returng. from settg. gin-traps and trip-guns before supper I encountered Half-Witted Jack and there immediately occurred to me one of the most ingenious Stratagems of my entire life, viz: to sell him the bent plough. This I did for the sum of 0£ 0s. 11½d., tellg. him, 'It is a new-fangled invention for tilling round fields.'

Percvg. a stout person wavg. a legal document at me I hastily returned to the Hall where I found Roderick and Willikins had celebrated the forthcomg. marriage. Roderick was unconscious by the fireplace in a pool of port, and Willikins in a similar condition. I joined their celebration with a bott. of Madeira, which I was consumg. when there came a wail from outside the window and a discordant bellow of drunken voices accompanied by violins with damp strings. Realising this was the Village Waits, who would demand money for their carols, I poured a bucket of water out of the window and they fled, leavg. behind two lanthorns and Short-

Sighted Samuel, who continued singing with his head buried in his music until I poured another bucket over him.

*Dec. 9*: Barnaby Toadstool attempted to stab himself but the knife broke. Pestilence raging in Barcelona. In a.m., whilst pursuing a poacher towards the Rectory I percvd. Half-Witted Jack stuck in the middle of a field and cryg. for help, hvg. ploughed the field in circles from the outside. Bt. horse cheap off Fredk. Hayseed. ITEM: To cheap horse 0£ 3s. 4¹/₄d.

Whilst on my way to evict Granny Turnip I encountered my old friend Sir Chas. Faggot, who wagered five sovs. that he could spit upon more undesirable persons than myself. I accepted in a trice and succeeded in expectoratg. upon fifteen Dissenters, three Papists and two foreigners, beatg. Sir Chas. by two Quakers and a Methodist. Exhilarated by my success, I crossed the road to spit upon a man who looked like a Jacobite, but upon my doing so he bowed and said, 'Thank you, sir, for coming across. I was just about to visit you,' and handed me a writ for debt. Whilst I was readg. this the dog spat upon me and hurried away.

When Sir Chas. expressed sympathy I tore up the writ and cried, 'Save your sorrow, Sir Chas! I no longer fear any writs, for my Roderick is to marry a lady with 10,000£ in the Funds in her own right!' This so impressed Sir Chas. that he asked me for a loan of 1,000£, although luckily I had wit enough to refuse. Dined at an inn upon a capon. As it was bad we threw it at the landlord.

Upon arrivg. home I retired early, exhausted by my efforts in the contest with Sir Chas. but was awoken at midnight by the sound of hooves and percvd. Roderick and Willikins being hoisted out of a cart and propped against the front door.

*Dec. 10*: Gales. Barnaby Toadstool killed when a tree fell on him. Great fire reported to be raging in Spitalfields. Horse which I bt. cheap off Fredk. Hayseed dropped dead in a.m.

*Dec. 11*: Rain. Mortalities: the Back, 4; the Bones, 1; the Bladder, 3; the Bowels, 5, By Own Hand, 1.

Since the season commenced I have been hunting frequently partly in pursuit of Reynard and partly in pursuit of Lady Emily Goodbody, widow of Sir Chas. Goodbody, who is reputed to use her whip as well in the bedchamber as in the chase, but have had little success as she is attacked by a fit of vomiting every time I approach, doubtless due to excess of emotion.

Went out again in a.m. but d—d poor sport. A great trumpeting and hallooing announced they had found Reynard near Ghoul's Covert but when we came up with the pack discovered they had been pursuing a vagrant whose pungent smell attracted the hounds. The wretched man climbed a tree and the hounds were called off with difficulty as they prefer the flesh of a vagrant to that of a fox, it being sweeter, although nothg. excites them more than the taste of a Quaker's leg, to which they seem peculiarly attracted.

*Dec. 12*: Fog. John Mungle died from the Shingles. No hunting today because of the weather. Very disappointing – we have had no eggs for a week as a fox has killed all the hens. Spent the a.m. playing cards with

Sir Jasper Fawcett. Lost 100 guineas.

Invited Sir Jasper to dine. Ate some smelts, boiled mutton, some fried chine and a tart made without eggs which tasted so vile I threw it at Grunge. Drank Madeira, claret, port, brandy and beer. Then to cards again. Lost 200 guineas. Drank more port and fell asleep in fireplace.

*Dec. 13*: Drizzle. John Shingle died from the Mungles. Awoke to find Sir Jasper asleep beside me and clutching my I.O.U. for 300 guineas. I tried to steal it but he awoke and cried, 'Ah, Haggard you had d—d bad luck last night. But I am in no hurry for payment – this evening will do.'

Hunted again in a.m. Not only does Lady Emily retch when I approach but now her horse is ill as well. Had asked the hunt to go over my own land today, hopg. to kill the fox that has eaten the hens, and pleased we found immediately. But the fox led us a dance and drawing away from the pack doubled back and ran past the field.

Seeing my last chance of eggs vanish I determined to stop him and drawg. a pistol from the saddle-bag let fly and settled Reynard's hash with a triumphant shout.

When the echoes of the shot had died away there was a terrible silence broken only by the sound of the Master of the Hunt sobbing. Then a chorus of curses and oaths broke out headed by Sir Jasper who bellowed, 'A man who shoots a fox is no gentln., sir. He is lower than a Whig, a Frenchman or even a Presbyterian. Sir, you are a scoundrel. Sir, I never wish to see you again. Sir, I swear from this day forth never to communicate with you in any way whatsoever, unless it be to horsewhip you.'

'In that case Sir Jasper,' I replied, 'you will presumably not ask for your 300 guineas,' with which I rode away in such a merry mood I forgot to kick a passing Dissenter.

*Dec. 14*: Gales. The Depression in Commerce is beginning to be felt strongly. Yesterday Ebenezer Firkin hanged himself because of a fall in the price of oats; and as I was passg. down the High St. Seth Horsetrough flung himself from an upper window with a cry of 'I am a ruined man! Death, I welcome thee.'

As chance would have it he landed not on the cobbles but upon a bailiff coming to repossess his house and while he was unhurt the bailiff was grievously injured. Nothwithstandg. he went off to purchase a knife that he might make sure next time.

How fortunate am I that the Depression in Trade will no longer affect me when Roderick is married. However, I am careful to keep close counsel over Roderick's anticipated wealth. If the news should leak out I will be besieged by persons wantg. money. He is not here at present, havg. left to stay with his friend Willikins but will return for Christmas.

For dinner ate a pigeon pie and a leg of mutton together with a piece of Grunge, who reached in front of my face just as I was grasping for a bone. The Haggards are known for the voracity of their appetite and being somewhat stupified with port I immediately took his hand in both of mine and gnawed it, findg. the flesh to taste somewhat putrid. Discovering my error from the vile flavour I flung away Grunge's member and upbraided the Miserable Domestick for lettg. his hand get in that condition; he deeply apologised and

explained he had just finished spreading some manure.
ITEM: Emeticks: 0£ 0s. 0¹/₂d.

*Dec. 16*: *The Intelligencer* reports that Gen. Burgoyne
is retreating in America. Doubtless he is luring the
rebellious Colonialists into a trap. To church in a.m.
Prayers said for His Majesty who has been attacked by
the Melancholick Distemper again and is said to have
mistaken Lord North for a chamber-pot and tried to
push him under the bed.

This day Roderick arrived home after a visit to the
home of Willikins in Warwickshire. Unfortunately, he
was speechless and insensible, doubtless from lack of
food on the journey, and Grunge and I tenderly carried
him to bed, or rather I carried my end tenderly  but
Grunge kept dropping his. Unfortunately, he was
holding Roderick's head.

*Dec. 17*: Fog. Mortalities: the Conniptions, 1; the
Copulation, 4. Ate some roast beef and pigs' trotters for
dinner. Also Roots. Afterwards the Rector called and
asked for money to distribute to the old and poor in the
parish at Christmas. Gave him 0£ 0s. 3¹/₂d. on
condition he will give nothg. to Crippled John until he
apologises for strikg. me with his crutch durg. the riots
against the Enclosure Acts. Also Grandpa Turnip, who
once voted against my man at an election.

Just before supper the Rector returned and said the
threepenny bit I gave him was bad, which I knew, havg.
received it from Surly Tom for a pig I sold him; but the
animal being diseased I thought it wiser not to say
anything.

Soon after breakfast came a Methody begging on

behalf of Decayed Gentlewomen; and he was followed by another seekg. money for slaves in Barbary and another asking alms for an orphanage until I told Grunge to answer the door no more. But then came a thunderous knockg. and I flung it open to be confronted by Perverted Polly, the whore from Lower Sodmire.

'Oh, sir,' she cried, 'If you have a heart give me some money to help poor Steaming Kathleen Malone. She is sinking fast with a fever caught from lying on the wet grass after the Hunt Supper and needs money for Physick. An old friend like you will not forget her in her need.'

'Nor shall I!' I cried. 'She did not forget me when I could not afford the usual threepence and I shall not forget her. I have no money, but return tomorrow, and I will raise it.'

*Dec. 18*: Out in a.m. to beg alms for Steaming Kathleen, but recvd. a cold welcome. The Rector refused to give anything, but the cantg. hypocrite said he would pray for her.

'Pray!' I ejaculated. 'That woman has given her health in the noblest service a woman could render her fellow human beings! Whilst you have been mouthg. hypocrisies on your knees, she has been servg. mankind on her back. Know you not she has been patronised by sevl. bishops and the Lord Lieutenant himself?'

But alas, it did no good, and my collection realised but two pieces of string, an old chestnut, four apples and a groat. Palsied Peter gave me a box containg. a shrivelled piece of human flesh, and asked me to give it to Kathleen so she would know what she had done to him.

On my returng. home Polly called to say Kathleen was worse and would I call a priest. My first impulse was to say I would as soon call Jack Ketch, but charity prevailed and I called on Father O'Flynn, a Papist who ministers to the Irish navigators buildg. the new canal and asked him to see Kathleen.

Sevl. hours later I was aroused by a knock on the door and there was Polly overjoyed. 'Sir,' she cried, 'All is well. As soon as the priest saw Kathleen he declared her the finest piece of flesh he had ever seen, even better than the Dublin whores, gave her a guinea and jumped into bed with her. She sent the money to the apothecary – he delivered the Physick – and she is now well again.'

'And the Priest?' I asked.

'Alas,' cried Polly, 'He succumbed to the exertion and has just been given the Last Rites. Oh sir, I am so grateful to you.'

ITEM: To Polly, for special services: 0£ 0s. 1¹/₂d.

*Dec. 20*: Roderick is in ecstasy because yesterday he recvd. a gift from his Beloved Miss Foulacre, together with an affectionate letter invitg. us to Foulacre Hall in January. Provided he does not mar everythg. by some act of stupidity, this could be the last Christmas in which I have to worry about money. Alas, the poor lad does not hv. all his wits about him (a quality he inherits from his mother) and is liable to do anything.

I believe we had an excellent dinner; unfortunately I cannot remember anythg. about it as I collapsed under the table after the first remove.

*Dec. 24*: Wind. Mortalities: The Paralytick Spasms, 3; The Putrid Fever, 2; The Purple Eruptions, 4; The Pox, 24.

Mindful that this is the season of goodwill I gathered the servants together and distributed Christmas gifts. To each and every one gave I a piece of coal and to Grunge a particularly large piece, since he has not been paid this year; Mrs. Runcible, the housekeeeper declined her lump saying she still had the piece I gave her last Christmas.

Grunge asked if he might have Mrs. Runcible's piece, as he was trying to save up enough for a fire in his room and in four or five years would have sufficient. I gladly consented and attended midnight service with a good heart and a clear conscience, although I fell over in front of the altar owing to faintness, having been so busy all day I had taken no nourishment except two botts. of brandy and a pail of port.

*Dec. 25*: Rain. This day being that most sacred feast in the Christian Calendar, viz: Quarter Day, I sallied forth in a.m. to evict those behind with their rents. The first tenant was old Granny Hayseed, who snivelled, 'Do you not know what day it is?' to which I replied, 'Yes, Rent Day,' which caused me so much mirth I nearly fell into an Apoplexy.

Altogether I evicted the largest number of tenants I have expelled since Christmas three years ago; including One-Armed Oswald, Club-Footed Cuthbert, Deaf Daniel, Impotent Isaac and Deformed Dorothy. By the time I reached the end of the street I was footsore and weary; then I realised they had all crept back into their houses when my back was turned. I was too tired to start again, so contented myself with trippg. up Blind Billy. As he has a malevolent turn of mind and might take revenge I snarled in a disguised voice, 'There is a present from Crippled John,' and returned to the Hall.

Shot a trespasser in p.m. After he fled I remembered it might have been my brother-in-law who sometimes walks over on Christmas Day. To dinner, a merry meal, with many toasts to Roderick's new Amour. Ate a goose, some bacon, a few brains, a boiled rabbit and a Puddg. My wife said, 'It is strange we have not seen my brother Jack this Christmas Day, he usually strolls over.'

Roderick asked, 'Why have you turned pale, father?' but I was preserved from my Dilemma by swooning from too much wine.

*Dec. 26*: Hail. Crippled John beaten by Blind Billy. Awoke late. Grunge came to me in a.m. to return the old breeches I gave him as a Christmas present. He said there was a huge hole in the fork. This I knew well, since the aperture had been bitten out by Lady Constance Bedwell in a moment of passion after the Hunt Ball last year. Upbraided the Snivellg. Lackey for his ingratitude to which he replied that it was just as well he was rejectg. the gift because he knew not what diseases he might have catched from the breeches.

Lay on my bed nearly all day, shootg. at tradesmen who approached the Hall with bills and succeeded in damaging a particularly obnoxious grocer.

# Chapter Three
## An Affair of Honour

*Dec. 31*: Rain. Artemus Birdseed died from an Excess of Drink over Christmas, he havg. wagered Wm. Turnip a penny that he could drink a bucket of ale without takg. it from his lips and did apparently succeed, draining the vessel before sinking to the floor insensible, never to rise again.

This being New Year's Eve I sat up with Roderick and struck by the solemnity of the occasion, that a new year was dawning which might bring we knew not what, I earnestly counselled him on the way to go in life.

'Remember, my son,' I cried, 'that life does not merely consist of drinking and fornication. There are other matters as we progress to the Great Tavern in the Sky. What they are eludes me at present but believe me they are none the less important for the fact I have forgotten them.

'And now my boy, let me give you the best piece of advice a doting father can give. Always carry a sixpence on a string round your neck in case you should meet a whore and not have the money to pay her. Here is the sixpence, with a hole bored in it ready. Promise me you will carry it always and remember that with economy it is enough for two whores.'

Roderick pledged to do so and we both toasted each other as I gazed on my son with pride, a credit to the Haggard line and Oxford University.

*Jan. 1, 1778*: Wind. Immediately midnight had struck we went outside to hear the New Year rung in, but instead of the merry ding-dong we expected there was a dull thud followed by silence and on runng. to the church we discovered the first pull on the bellropes had brought down the belfry, which had not been repaired since it was damaged by Roundheads in the Civil War. Unfortunately the Rector was not injured but alas, Zeke Barnworthy was killed by the Great Tenor Bell. He owed me a halfpenny, which I shall never see again.

On arisg. in a.m. I sat down to make a list of resolutions in this New Year and compiled the followg., viz:

To pray every day for the victory of the gallant Gen. Burgoyne over the Rebellious Americans.

To forgive my enemies, always exceptg. those such as Frenchmen.

To be constantly vigilant for Papist plots against our lawful King and to watch carefully for signs of a Jacobite rebellion in the village.

Not to do my imitation of Louis XVI on his honeymoon night more than twice in one eveng.

Not to have a whore more than once a week, and then only a threepenny one.

To live like an English gentln. and honour God and The King.

*Jan. 6*: Frost. The full toll of Parish Mortalities over the 12 days of Christmas is as follows, viz: killed jumpg. off the church roof after drinkg. the Rector's mulled wine, 1; choked tryg. to consume too much food, 7; hit over head by their wives, 2; the Bowels, 1; the Bile, 2; the Bells, 1 (Zeke Barnworthy).

*Jan. 8*: Frost. The weather continues v. cold. Met an interestg. gentln. in the Red Lion Inn called Munchausen. He told me that when the mail coach from London passed along the turnpike, the guard blew his horn in the usual manner but no sound came forth as the notes had frozen inside the horn. Later, when the coach stopped to change horses at Lower Sodmire, he rested the horn by the fireplace whereupon it thawed out and the notes suddenly came forth by themselves and a fanfare sounded.

He said this was vouched for by many witnesses and their testimony could not have been affected by lack of nourishment as they had all just consumed a quart of hot punch to keep out the cold.

*Jan. 9*: Prester Kneebone d. from Spontaneous Combustion, the first case reported in the district since Queen Anne's time. As he was in the High St. at the time of his immolation, three cottages were burnt to the ground but thank God, none belonged to me.

*Jan. 10*: Saw sevl. amusg. executions in a.m. The hangman was in a merry mood and when his foot went through a rotten plank on the scaffold he animadverted thus, viz: 'A plague on these rotten gallows. They will kill somebody some day.' A collection for the hangman raised 0£, 0s. 3½d.

Later went to jeer at people in the stocks, especially Dismal Desmond, who once cheated me out of a penny.

Amused myself by makg. rude gestures and then threw an egg at him, but he threw it back and it landed on my wig.

Ate some boiled beef, boiled rabbit and calves' brains for dinner. There was only a small portion of brains: I was about to remark to my wife that from the smallness of the portion they must have belonged to a female animal when I became aware she had picked up a tureen of soup and remarked 'Pray say it, Mr. Haggard. Do not keep silent on my account.' I therefore deemed it wiser to keep silent, it being well-known the Female Sex possess inordinate strength when roused.

*Jan. 11*: Prester Kneebone buried. As the coffin was being lowered into the grave, his remains burst into flames a second time, the coffin exploded and the mourners fled.

*Jan. 16*: Wm. Lightfinger struck dead by an Act of God, he havg. stolen a penny from the church poor-box by putting his penknife in the slot.

This day Roderick and I set forth to visit Sir Josh. Foulacre and to restore our fortunes. My wife Tib could not travel because of the Bile, but shrieked advice and abuse as we drove away. On passg. through the gates I succeeded in driving down a Dissenting Preacher, which I took as a good omen for our visit and we sped towards Foulacre Hall along the turnpike.

'When we return,' said Roderick 'we shall be rich for life.'

*Jan. 17*: Rain. Mad Jacob tried to walk across the new canal and was drowned. As a wheel of the coach fell off whilst we pursued a Papist along the road, we did not arrive until midnight and had no opportunity to form an impression of Foulacre Hall until the morning. It is even larger than I had hoped and there are strong evidences of wealth.

At breakfast we met the family. Fanny Foulacre is a mature lady of about twenty-nine (some eight years older than Roderick), the regularity of whose features is marred by sevl. warts on her face. But she is tall and has a good figure, includg. a bosom of such strikg. proportion that I was compelled to warn Roderick not to stare at it durg. breakfast. Her mother is a lady of a certain age, yet extremely desirable. She is Fanny's stepmother in fact, Sir Josh. hvg. married again on the death of his first wife. Sir Josh. himself is short and white-haired, with a red complexion and piercg. blue eyes and of immense width across the chest and shoulders.

Sir Josh. showed me the grounds in a.m., durg. which a singular incident occurred, viz: whilst passg. through a covert we surprised a poacher in the trees. Instead of arrestg. him Sir Josh. said: 'D— you, you d—d poachg. rascal, you hv. interrupted our promenade. I cannot waste time to take you to the Constable. Will you fight me, man to man?'

At this the low creature's face brightened, since he was a big, powerful person, and he replied, 'If you will fight fair I will. I have never hit a gentln. before, but I reckon they go down as easy as other folks. And you promise, mind, I shall go free after we have fought?'

'D— you, you need not query a gentln.'s word,' shouted Sir Josh. 'Come on then and be d—d to you, as I am in a hurry.'

With this exchange of pleasantries they fell to. But

the fight, if such it could be called, lasted but a moment The poacher aimed a mighty blow at Sir Josh., which he parried, despite his short stature. He then smote the poacher in the stomach and when he doubled up raised both fists and struck him smartly on the back of the neck. Finally, he picked up the wretched fellow and rendered him unconscious by thrustg. his head against a tree sevl. times. After which he threw him over the hedge into the road as if he had weighed no more than a baby, and continued the walk.

At this exposition of strength I decided to tread warily in any dealgs. with Sir Josh.

Roderick was engaged in playg. cards with his Enamoured and peerg. furtively at her bosom the while. I took him aside and impressed upon him that it would be fatal if his natural impatience to enjoy the Fruits of Passion led him to anticipate the Lawful Rites of Marriage, which would ruin all our plans.

'And from the appearance of Sir Josh. it would earn us a broken neck a-piece as well,' I added.

As an example to Roderick, and to impress Sir Josh. that his daughter was marryg. into a family of gentln., I drank two quarts of Madeira at dinner to demonstrate I could hold my liquor, and was most careful to expectorate only in the fireplace. I praised Sir Josh. and his wife, Fanny, the Hall and anythg. else I could find to lie about. Unfortunately Roderick, thinkg. to emulate me, and tryg. to flatter Miss Fanny, told her father he thought she had the finest Bum he had seen outside of London.

'And there are some very fine ones there,' he added with a leer.

At this Sir Josh. said loudly, 'Perhaps you are

fatigued and wish to retire?'

I protested we had never felt livelier, but Sir Josh. took up a candlestick and personally escorted Roderick and myself to our rooms. As we mounted the stairs, I percvd. on the landg. a splendid pair of silver-mounted pistols on the wall, together with two swords. I asked Sir Josh. if he were afraid of thieves. He replied he was afraid of no man, nor any beast either. They were his duellg. weapons.

'I have killed five men with those pistols,' he said 'and two more with the swords. Aye, and wounded three others so much they'll never walk again. And I regretted not one of them. For the dogs had insulted a lady in my presence.

At this Roderick started to tremble and after Sir Josh. had bade us goodnight he cried, 'This is a fine pickle we are in when a man might be run through by his father-in-law!' But I counselled patience and once more warned him not to gaze with such ardour at Miss Fanny's delicious protuberances, unless he wished to incur Sir Josh.'s wrath.

*Jan. 18*: Hail. Attended church in a.m. with a serene mind, Sir Josh. havg. invited us to worship in a manner which brooked no refusal. Roderick amused himself by drawing sketches in his hymn book until I looked at him, whereupon he ogled his Loved One.

At dinner the entire family gathered, some twenty persons in all, includg. sevl. aged aunts, uncles and numerous half-witted cousins. Percvg. a mere 20 botts. of wine amongst this vast throng I secured four or five botts. for myself in case of a shortage, but Sir Josh. called out, 'Sir, I fear you were under a misapprehension at dinner yesterday. In this house moderation in all things is considered a virtue, a sentiment with which I am sure you agree.' I forced my features into a smile, privily d—g him for a d—d cantg. hypocritical dog, and sipped my wine genteely, concealg. a bott. between my knees.

After dinner we sat round in the family circle. D—d dull. One of the aged uncles swooned from eatg. too much and had to be bled. Sir Josh. suggested a contest at Grinng. Through a Hoop, which was won by his Great-Aunt, whose face is permanently fixed in a hideous leer due to an attack of the Palsy. Afterwards the younger cousins played Blind Man's Buff.

Thinkg. to brighten the proceedgs. I cried, 'Let us have some of the good old merry japes and sports with which we enliven the winter back home at Haggard Hall!'

'By all means,' said Sir Josh. lookg. down his nose sourly, 'as long as Decorum and Sensibility are not offended.'

'Of course,' I said. 'But what could be more innocent or conducive to Merriment than a contest As To Whom Can Expectorate the Farthest?'

I immediately lined up all the ladies across the room and explained the rules. As there appeared some reluctance to begin, I demonstrated my full strength at this Noble Art and succeeded in reachg. the mirror above the fireplace.

At this Sir Josh. coughed loudly and said, 'Perhaps somethg. less strenuous might be more appropriate for the occasion? I would suggest a game of riddles.'

Desirous of impressg. the company that Roderick's father was a man of wit I instantly volunteered the followg. conundrum: 'why is the Bishop of Durham like a French whore?'* As nobody volunteered the answer, I was about to give it myself when the most astoundg. event occurred, viz: there was a scream from the room above and a shower of plaster fell from the ceilg. This was followed by a rendg. noise and a human foot appeared near the chandelier.

A glance round the room confirmed that Roderick was not there, and fearing the worse I ran hastily upstairs, but was outdistanced by Sir Josh. who burst into Roderick's bedroom to reveal Roderick vainly tryg. to extract his foot from a rotten floorboard into which he had sunk, whilst Fanny lay on the bed with her dress in such disarray that one bosom was exposed, screamg. loudly, 'I am undone!'

*Jan. 19*: Rain. Eli Seaweed d. from Gripg. of the Guts. Upon enterg. the room, Sir Josh. stood speechless for a moment and I hoped he might drop dead from an Apopletick Seizure. But he recovered and shouted, 'Miss, go to your room, this instant, d'ye hear? The Doctor shall examine you later and if you are not as you were, by G——, you shall spend the rest of your life in a nunnery, by G——!' He then turned to Roderick as if to speak, but instead gave a terrible snarl and left the chamber. After extricatg. Roderick's foot from the floor, as a result of which the chandelier below crashed to the ground, we deemed it safer to remain together rather than risk a venture downstairs and the chance of meetg. Sir Josh. on the rampage.

Roderick explained that his Natural Feelgs. had over-

* The answer cannot be found – Ed.

come my stern warng. Seized by an Overmasterg.
Passion he had asked Miss Fanny to show him the
house, and as he was passg. his room he dragged her
inside and foolishly endeavoured with all his might to
anticipate the Lawful Rites.

'And if the d—d bitch hadn't been so coy and led me
such a dance that I put my foot through the floor a-
chasing her, I'd have had my will upon her,' he said.

*Jan. 20*: We passed a sleepless night. At seven o'clock
in a.m. a servant knocked on the door and presented the
followg. note, viz: 'Sir Josh. presents his compliments
to Mr Amos and Roderick Haggard and regrets that
pressg. business prevents his joing. them for breakfast,
which they will doubtless wish to take immediately
upon receipt of this communication, so as to leave at the
earliest possible moment. He further wishes to state
that in his opinion certain remarks of Mr Haggard
senior the previous night could be construed as being
insultg. to the ladies, and that the behaviour of Mr
Haggard jnr. towards his daughter must be construed in
the same light. He therefore takes the liberty of enclosg.
his card and informg. both gentln. that his second will
wait upon them at Haggard Hall and that he hopes
neither of them will deny him the satisfaction due from
one gentln. to another.'

The receipt of this dire missive threw me into such
distress that I only recovd. by applyg. myself to a bott.
of brandy which I always carry. Upon lowerg. the bott. I
percvd. Roderick had fainted clean away and I was
obliged to burn feathers under his nose before he could
be aroused. As he regained consciousness there was a
loud knock at the door and he fainted away again, cryg.

44

out as he fell, 'Mercy! I do not wish to die!', but it was only a servant with a tray and two dishes of chocolate.

He informed us our coach was waitg. and Sir Josh. would be vastly obliged if we would excuse his not attendg. us, as he would be 'engaged in sword practice'.

We wasted no more time but on the instant quitted Foulacre Hall. As we passed down the drive I percvd. Sir Josh. standg. in front of a tree to which was attached a dummy dressed in clothes remarkably like mine. He was thrustg. at the dummy with his sword and cryg. 'Insult a lady would you? Then take that – and that – and that'; with which he pierced the dummy in the bowels with such force that the blade stuck in the tree. As we drove out of sight I saw him take a pair of pistols and shoot down two birds in the air. We then drove home hastily, stoppg. only to jeer at a Methodist preacher on the turnpike.

On arrival at Haggard Hall my wife greeted us, cryg. 'When is the happy day to be then?'

Upon my informg. her that there would be no happy day, but every likelihood of a v. unhappy one tomorrow, she shouted 'You stupid Ninnies!' and began to belabour Roderick with a broomstick, at which I took the opportunity to make my escape to the Buttery, where I have concealed a privy store of Fortified Cordial Waters against such unpleasant events. ITEM: To Cherry Brandy 0£ 1s. 6d.

*Jan. 21*: Blizzards. Chas. Sideboard poisoned by his Wife. Weird William suffocated by Maniacal Michael. Feelg. it wiser to absent myself from the Hall in case of an approach by Sir Josh. I took Roderick out on business. Evicted Crippled John, Palsied Pete and

Mumblg. Myrtle. In p.m. percvd. interestg. funeral, and upon enquirg. whom was the Deceased, was informed it was Wm. Drain, of Vulture-sub-Underwood. This distressed me greatly, as he owed me 0£. 0s. 1³/₄d. for some hay, and had always boasted he would never pay as he says I once sold him a sheep which had the staggers. As the coffin was lowered into the grave, therefore, I fired a charge from my fowlg.-piece at the mourners, at which they dropped it with a loud crash and jumped into the grave after it.

Just before dark, crossg. the Park in search of poachers, I percvd. a pair of moleskin breeches stickg. out of a bush and gave them a charge from my horse-pistol, whereupon it transpired they were occupied by my keeper Mellors, who had been set upon by a gang of poachers and thrust into the bush. I threw him into a nearby pond to cool his wounds, and gave him a piece of coal which I always carry with me, to compensate for his injuries. I then tied him to a tree as a human lure and surrounded him with gin-traps, which would ensnare the poachers when they returned. Unfortunately, I drank five botts. of Canary at supper in order to forget Sir Josh. and fell asleep without returng.

*Jan. 22*: Rain. Witless Walter tried to fly from the top of the church and d. instantly.

Soon after breakfast there was a thunderous knock at the front door. I was about to hide under a bed when a smart-look. gentln. strode in and said, 'My name is Fairfax, sir. I am Sir Josh. Foulacre's second in this little matter between yourself and your son and him. Sir Josh. will wait upon you here at 6.30 tomorrow morning and upon your son a few minutes afterwards. Perhaps you would care to give me the name of your second?'

For a moment I was unable to reply but eventually remarked I would act as Roderick's second and he as mine, whereupon Fairfax replied, 'That is not possible sir, as it is unlikely you will survive the first encounter to assist in the second. As you know, Sir Josh. is the finest shot in five counties. However, I shall leave the choice to you.' With which he bowed courteously and quitted the room.

When I recovered my wits I immediately shouted for Roderick and told him the news; at which he fainted away and could only be revived with brandy-and-water. A quart of the life-givg. restorative havg. been administered we discussed what to do.

Whether we fought Sir Josh. or not he would revenge himself I had no doubt; therefore flight was our only resource. Called my wife Tib and told her what had happened; she said she would go to her sister. Informed Grunge he was to look after the house and say we had gone he knew not where, when there was a loud knock on the door and a shout of 'Open in the name of the Law!'

At this we stayed not a moment longer but fled out the back and hid in the kitchen garden, leavg. Grunge to deal with the callers. After half-an-hour he came into the garden and pausg. by our hidg.-place whispered, 'They are officers of the court come to arrest you for debt. Sir, and take you away for same.'

Told Grunge to bring round horses to the wicket gate and we would escape, but just then two men ran from the house shoutg. 'Halt! You are discovered. Halt in the King's name!'

All would have gone hard with us had not faint cries

from the covert a hundred yards away reminded me Mellors was still tied to a tree. I told Roderick to run for the covert with all speed and on enterg. led him past the gin-traps and spring-guns and out the other side. As we emerged cries of pain from the pursuers announced the ruse had succeeded. We stopped only to cut Mellors free. He was unable to speak but his honest eyes were full of gratitude and such was his emotion he appeared to spit at me, but I believe he was tryg. to lick my hand.

After restg. a moment, we began to hasten along the road with the intention of puttg. as much distance between ourselves and Haggard Hall as possible, when we came up with a horse and cart being driven by Half-Witted Jack. I commanded him to stop and tellg. him we were being pursued asked him to drive on whilst we hid ourselves under the hay in the cart.

He made no reply to this request, but after starg. at me for a long time said, 'You'm be the gentln. as sold me a bent plough yesterday sennight.' I assured him that bent ploughs were all the mode; notwithstandg. he persisted in his crafty manner, 'And Oi heard yew laughin' at me when Oi ploughed up the glebe and got stuck in the middle.'

Realisg. that his feeble wits had taken a malevolent turn I felt in my pocket and fetched out a shillg. which I gave to him, whereupon he told us to get in and hide ourselves and not to stir until he gave the word.

We were about an hour under the hay when the cart stopped and there was the sound of voices. Fearg. that the officers had stopped the cart we remained hidden, although I was forced to put my hand over Roderick's mouth to stop him blubberg. with fear. Suddenly, how-ever, the cart was tilted back by the shafts and before we could save ourselves we slid out into the parish pond to the sound of much mirth from sevl. onlookers, amongst whom I recognised Eph. Snail who sold me a diseased sheep last Candlemas.

Half-Witted Jack shouted that would teach me to go round sellg. honest folk bent ploughshares, whilst Mad Jane screeched, 'Aye, and every girl in the village knows he has a bent ploughshare himself,' at which there was further unseemly mirth.

Lest the officers should be watchg. the turnpike we escaped by side-roads and spent the night at an ale-house. ITEM: To spendg. night in alehouse 0£ 0s. 1½d.; Ale, 0£ 5s. 3½d.

*Jan. 23*: Rain. Wheezing Wilfred poisoned by Vile Vincent. Simple Sydney hit himself on the head with a hammer to see what it felt like, and d. instantly. In a.m. we held a council. Return to Haggard Hall is impossible for fear of arrest for me and death for both of us at the hands of Sir Josh. We therefore decided to take sanctuary with my cousin Roger Haggard, who lives in the fair city of Bath, and repair our fortunes as best we could. I had my purse containg. seven sovs. in my pocket, and Roderick had two more. These would pay for our journey. So we set out at once in a carrier's cart for a town some miles distant, where we might take the Bath coach.

*Jan. 24*: Wind. Took coach in a.m. travellg. outside to save money. The further we removed from Sir Josh. the more sanguine we became. A gentln. on the coach told me it is reported that the French are digging a tunnel under the Channel with the intention of infiltrating numbers of priests, who will convert the English populace to Rome. The tunnel is only three feet high so it is being dug by dwarves and the French bishops are recruitg. stunted priests. Queen Marie Antoinette has visited the workings and distributed cake to the workmen. Is there no end to foreign perfidy?

I decided that if the French should invade I shall gain time for flight by askg. Grunge to make a gallant sacrifice of himself; if that fails I shall ask my wife to offer herself to the French officer. This will bring on an attack of vomiting, during which I shall escape.

Thus the time passed pleasantly until towards eveng. we came in sight of the City of Bath.

# Chapter Four
## Taking the Waters

*Jan. 25*: Fog. The Rev. Septimus Sneer, of Bath, struck dead whilst composg. a Treatise Upon Eternal Life. It was after midnight when we arrived at the house of my cousin Roger, although a fashionable rout was still in progress there. We announced ourselves to a footman and asked for my cousin, but the footman said, 'I regret sir, that the Master has just been carried to his bed insensible after fallg. downstairs in pursuit of a young female.'

The servant, however, recognised me from a previous visit (as well he might, for he had stolen 0£ 6s. 8$^{1/2}$d. off me whilst I was drunk). He therefore allowed us to enter and showed us a room where we spent the night.

Upon awakeng. I counted my money, as is my habit, and found the servant had stolen a further 0£ 0s. 7$^{3/4}$d. from me. My cousin rose late after his debauch of the night before, so Roderick and I took stock whilst we waited his arrival. We have between us 0£ 11s. 6d. in money and the sixpence which Roderick keeps round his neck on a piece of string, in case he should meet a desirable whore and not have money to pay her. That is the sole amount of our worldly wealth and we dare not return to Haggard Hall whilst the writs for debt still run and Sir Josh. is intent upon killg. us. We therefore agreed to throw ourselves upon Cousin Roger's mercy until such time as we could mend our fortunes and fend for ourselves.

We occupied ourselves with the paper until eleven o'clock, studyg. lists of parish mortalities and reports of Plague in various parts. At that hour my cousin came downstairs with his head in a wet turban and greeted us as warmly as his condition allowed. 'You are welcome to be my guests for a *brief* while, after which you will doubtless prefer to make other arrangements,' he said, to which I replied that his own last *brief* visit to Haggard Hall had lasted three months. He would have replied but turned pale and was helped upstairs again.

Roderick and I then sallied forth to spy out the land. Whilst strollg. up Milsom Street we ogled numerous members of the Fair Sex and Roderick declared, 'I have never seen a greater quantity of excellent female flesh gathered together in one place before.' I impressed upon him that our chief hope lay in one of us makg. a profitable liaison, whether marriage or otherwise, whereupon he began to whine and claimed *he* had made a profitable connection.

'All would have been well if you had not enraged Sir Josh. by gobbg. in the fireplace,' he said unjustly. However, I made no reply to this as I must not give Roderick cause for the Sulks. Later we visited the Pump Room where I discovered that its evil-tasting Chalybeate Waters can be made palatable by the infusion of equal quantities of brandy from my flask. Ate one pigeon pie between the two of us for dinner, to save money, but Roderick's half was bad. In p.m. to Assembly Rooms and played cards, chiefly whist owg. to lack of money. By usg. our well-tried system of signallg. to each other, viz: The Haggard Patent Telegraph, which consists of signs made by wavg. a back-scratcher, we won 11 sovs., enough to provide our needs for sevl. days. I then increased our capital by wagerg. a gentln. at the table, the Hon. Cholmondley-Fitzroy, two sovs. that I could name the card he held in his hand, and won, Roderick hvg. signalled what it was.

*Jan. 26*: Sleet. Bart. Oakroyd believed the Evil Eye was on him and d. instantly. An American Colonialist named Benj. Franklin is reported to have burst into flames whilst flyg. a kite in a thunderstorm. Insulted elderly Baptist in a.m. and in p.m. visited Assembly Rooms, where we took up again with the Hon. Chol-mondley-Fitzroy, off whom we won no less than 200 sovs. at cards without hvg. to cheat, as he is totally devoid of any wits whatsoever. Cards being over, he called some of the Fancy to meet me, and begged me to demonstrate a few merry wagers, whereupon I wagered all six of his friends five sovs. they could not drink a glass of wine whilst standg. on their heads. They hvg. failed to do so, I stood on my own head and performed the feat with the aid of a straw. ITEM: To glasses, 0£ 0s. 11d.

Encouraged by my success I drank five pints of Chalybeate Water and brandy, whilst Roderick roamed the town in search of a whore, I hvg. given him 0£ 0s. 3$^{1}/_{2}$d. for the purpose. 'And bring back any change you might receive from the wench,' I told him sternly, 'as money is precious in our straitened circumstances.'

The drink stimulated my amorous propensities and I began to glance round the room at the white bosoms of the women when my glance fell upon a bosom of exceptional rotundity. Upon enquirg. the fortunate owner I was informed it was the Lady Amelia Farthingale. Her husband, who is old, being prostrated by gout she was attended only by a maid and I instantly introduced myself.

'Madam,' I cried, bowg. so low that my knee-breeches nearly split up the back, 'I believe I have the honour of addressg. the Lady Amelia Farthingale? We met at Cheltenham.'

She looked at me for a moment in surprise and then said languidly, 'Indeed, sir, I believe we did. Is it not Mr. er…er…?' From this I knew her to be no inexperienced campaigner in the Wars of Cupid, and we were soon in the most animated intercourse.

I pressed her to drink and encouraged her to consume about half a gall. of punch, which I had privily fortified with brandy. We then danced a spirited quadrille, durg. which I took the opportunity to squeeze her hand and gaze into her eyes and announce I would die for her. She replied, 'La, sir, you are too bold, I am a married woman.' However, she did not leave, not even when under the influence of the brandy I fell over in a dance and slid 20 feet on my back.

At the conclusion of the proceedgs. she informed me her companion had disappeared and she would be glad of my company to escort her home. I instantly ordered a chair for her and followed to her lodgs. in Great Pulteney Street, my emotions being aroused to such an extent I could scarce articulate to abuse the chair-men. Paid the chair-men with trembling hands, givg. each an additional 0£ 0s. 1³/₄d., as I know from experience that if not rewarded they would have created a disturbance which might have aroused the house and thwarted my desires. Lady Amelia said not a word, but led me in through a back staircase and thence up to her room, although I panted so hard with excitement that I could hardly mount the stairs.

*Jan. 27*: Rain. Whilst sufferg. from the Melancholick Distemper, His Majesty the King is reported to have mistaken Lord North for a wardrobe & tried to hang his coat on him. Last night occurred one of the greatest events of our age, viz: I was privileged to debauch a Lady of Quality, the first woman of rank I have enjoyed for seven years. I had scarce entered the room before I was enjoying the Felicities of her Person.

'Madam, my passion for you is overwhelmg.,' I cried and she replied, 'O, Mr. Haggard, you are irresistible!'

Memory fails to record the number of times we conjoined in the Lists of Venus, fallg. apart breathless like spent swimmers and then, hvg. refreshed ourselves with a quart of negus, hurlg. ourselves anew into the tender fray. Lady Amelia exhibited the greatest tokens of delight at my embraces. Indeed, the enthusiasm of her amorous activity on one occasion caused us to fall out of bed. Fortunately her husband, owg. to his gout, sleeps downstairs, and takes laudanum. ITEM: To repair of bed, 0£ 0s. 6$^{1}/_{2}$d.

I arose early, and stole stealthily down the back-stairs before the house was awake, havg. arranged with my Beloved to meet her that evening. I then returned to my cousin's house and awoke Roderick to tell him the news. But he had a Fit of Vapours and sulked. He told me he had given a girl 0£ 0s. 3d. in King's Mead Fields, and upon recvg. the money she fled, he being unable to follow her as his breeches were round his knees.

'Do not worry,' I told him. 'Our fortunes are made. Your Father has secured for himself a Lady of the First Rank with a rich husband and doubtless we shall both enjoy the fruits of the liaison in golden sovs., and then you shall have another threepence – nay, sixpence – for a girl.'

After dinner I once more sallied forth to the Assembly Rooms, where I won 50 sovs. at bezique with the Hon. Cholmondley-Fitzroy. Won a further 25 sovs. wagerg. I could drink a pint of port in ten secs. ITEM: To Emeticks: $0£$ 0s. $0^{1}/_{4}$d. My impatience to see my Beloved and once more enter those sweetest of wars, the Battles of Aphrodite, was so great I could scarce conceal my anxiety; indeed, I accidentally dealt Lord Butterwick a hand containg. two Aces of Spades, one being a spare concealed in my cuff.

As time passed, and there was no sign of my Fair One, I became anxious, until about eleven o'clock her maid arrived and gave me a note which said: 'I cannot come tonight. My husband is suspicious. But come with my maid to the house after midnight, when he has taken his laudanum.'

The magic hour hvg. struck I commandeered a chair and was conveyed to the house, where her maid showed me the back-stairs as before. My Amelia was already in bed, a gallon of negus by her side and her complexion a roseate hue. A faint snorg. sound announced that Morpheus, as well as Venus had claimed my Love, and it was with some difficulty I aroused her by throwg. a jug of water in her face. She explained that she had had recourse to her favourite stimulant, orange cordials mixed with negus, and as a consequence had fallen asleep.

While she was still speakg. I tore off my clothes and leaped into bed with such velocity that one of the legs collapsed. Notwithstandg. this interruption, I once more sallied forth into the Tournament of Venus with all the ardour of a young knight. My fair companion displayed the greatest felicity at my efforts, addressg. me as 'My Hero', 'My Jupiter' and similar epithets of a flatterg. nature. Once more I joined in the wars of the Paphian Queen times without number. Such was the vigour of our conjoinment that on one ***********

*Editor's Note: The manuscript is indecipherable here through blots, almost certainly the effects of Haggard's drooling.*

******and on another occasion my fellow-worshipper at the shrine of Venus bit my toe with such vigour that I let out a loud cry which I feared must have awoken the neighbourhood.

I arose at dawn, and bestowg. a last kiss on the form of my Beloved, who was again deep in the arms of Morpheus, stole from the room and returned to my cousin's house. Found Roderick had fallen asleep whilst tryg. to climb the stairs, so I had to kick him awake.

*Jan. 28*: Blizzards. Saw unusual hanging in a.m., the executioner fallg. off the scaffold and breakg. his neck, to the great delight of the crowd, many of whom uttered cries of 'encore' and similar witticisms. Saml. Grind ate a toadstool and expired.

Exhilarated by my success in the Fields of Amorous Dalliance I visited the Pump Rooms, where I fortified myself with Chalybeate Waters and brandy before playg. cards. Nothg. could go wrong. Our luck was unusually high. Roderick, imbibg. too freely of wine, caused me the greatest alarm by drunkenly announcg., 'I will wager 100£ with anyone in the room that the next card will be an ace,' not realisg. I had already dealt the ace I keep up my sleeve.

Three gentln., includg. the Hon. Cholmondley-Fitzroy, accepted the wager and I was forced to deal the card without any opportunity of usg. a Stratagem. Our good fortune, however, was in such ascendant that it turned out to be an ace, and Cholmondley-Fitzroy cried, 'Haw, haw, haw, but you're a d—d lucky fellow Haggard and I don't know how you do it, by George.'

After this benison of Dame Luck Roderick and I celebrated by imbibg. freely. My own spirits were even more exhilarated by the thoughts of the female charms that were to be exposed to me later that night, when I proposed to ask Lady Amelia for a loan of 1,000£. Such was the intoxication of the wine, the cordials, the brandy and my good fortune that I amused myself by writg. on the wall: 'All lusty lads who wish for a good time should repair to the chambers of Lady Amelia Farthingale in Pulteney Street, where they will find their every want supplied.'

I then diverted the company by standg. on a table and shoutg. out sevl. witty toasts, viz: 'Here's to Lady Amelia Farthingale, the wealthiest whore in Bath'; and, 'I give you Lord Farthingale, who loaned me his wife.' At this I placed my fingers on my forehead in the manner of cuckold's horns, a gesture which caused the Hon. Cholmondley-Fitzroy to laugh so much he choked. Whilst deliverg. the latter toast I observed a strange silence had fallen upon the company. Upon my enquirg. the reason a fellow standg. near said, 'Her husband has just entered the room with five servants.'

At this I deemed it better to leave immediately; I had not gone five yards down the street when I was felled to the ground by a blow from behind and knocked insensible. I recovered to find myself in some sort of sack, tied hand and foot and apparently on the back of a cart. I called for help, but was kicked violently and told to be silent, or worse would befall me. After some minutes the cart stopped and I felt myself being lifted out and carried some distance. My bearers then stopped and I was swung to and fro three times before flyg. through the air to land in the River Avon where the current carried me away. My past life flashed before my eyes. How much I regretted I should never get revenge on Deaf Robin for sellg. me that diseased heifer or be able to distrain on Granny Brown. For a moment the air trapped in the sack buoyed me up and this saved my life, as the stream carried me on to a patch of mud at the side of the river. I have referred to the voracious appetite of the Haggards and this stood me in good stead now. By prodigious efforts I was able to gnaw a hole in the sack and work my head free.

I called for help and was surprised when a familiar voice answered; Roderick had seen me seized and followed my assailants. He now stood on the bank wringing his hands like a despoiled virgin.

It took some time to persuade him to advance into the water and drag me ashore and then only when I promised him a guinea. But eventually he did so and I collapsed on the grass while he capered away with the guinea all muddy as he was. He soon returned with a chair in which I was conveyed to our lodgings and then sallied forth to spend his guinea on a woman but the wench took not only his money but his watch as well.

*Jan. 29*: Rain. Gen. Burgoyne reported to have retreated again from the American Colonialists.* The Coroner has sat upon the hangman and decided that he died from fallg. off the scaffold. The events of the previous night hvg. induced a fever in me I spent the day in my room.

At noon a footman arrived, bearg. the followg. letter, viz: 'The Master of the Ceremonies presents his compliments and desires to inform Mr Haggard that owing to certain peculiarities of his Deportment, viz: Expectoratg. in the Chalybeate Well, dancing the quadrille with a bottle on his head, writing ladies' names and addresses on the walls, and paying bills in Birmingham Sovereigns,† Mr Haggard's absence will be preferred to his company until such time as he is prepared to mend his manners.'

Had this news come earlier it might hv. distressed me, but my good fortune at gamblg. had enabled us to gain sufficient money for our temporary needs. I nevertheless deemed it wiser not to visit the Assembly Rooms that eveng. but instead sallied forth to a private Rout, despite the lack of an invitation. Meanwhile I despatched Roderick to seek Lady Amelia's companion and find what had become of my Fair Coadjutor in the Rites of Love. He returned at midnight with the news that Lady Amelia and her husband had left Bath that day to return to London.

*General Burgoyne had, of course, already surrendered. But news travelled slowly in those days – Ed.
† i.e. forgeries

Although distressed to no longer enjoy the favours of my Sweet Amelia (nor be able to borrow 1,000£ from her) it was gratifying to hear they had departed, as I was now safe from further revenges by hired ruffians. I therefore celebrated the news by makg. a simple wager with some young gentln. of the Corinthian style in the room, viz: that I could belch longer and louder than anybody else present. Sevl. young bloods took up the challenge and the room soon resounded to the sound of our wager being executed with such vigour that our host requested us to leave as we were distressg. the ladies. Although not before I had won with a raspg. effort of unusual duration. This was so loud that the Watch came up and knocked on the door, thinkg. there had been a murder. ITEM: To the windy powders, 0£ 0s. 1³/₄d.

*Jan. 30*: Mist. Mordecai Jones sold his wife to a tinker for 3d. I rose late, still feelg. the effects of my involuntary immersion in the river, and thought it prudent, in view of my enfeebled state, to drink brandy for breakfast rather than risk the debilitatg. effects of hot chocolate or tea. Although gaing. strength rapidly, I was still not fully recovd., for when I aimed a kick at one of the servants, he dodged the blow, and I swung round and fell on my back. However, I took revenge later by droppg. a breakfast tray on his head from the top of the stairwell. ITEM: To teapot 0£ 0s. 4¹/₂d.

Whilst Roderick visited a circulatg. library in a.m. in order to borrow a novel, I read the *Bath Mercury*. I had just finished reading an account of an interestg. execution when my eye was drawn to a large advertisement at the sight of which the blood rushed to

my head and I nearly swooned. The advertisement was
as follows, viz:

*In the matter of Amos Haggard, Esq., Worm.*
*(And his son Roderick, also Worm)*
A Reward of 100£ is offered for information leading to news
of the whereabouts of the above by a gentleman Whom they have
insulted and to Whom they have refused Satisfaction.

Amos Haggard is of middle age, and medium stature. His
complexion is purple and he has a wart on his chin. His son
Roderick is a pallid, snivelling youth much given to tears and
women.

Both of them were last heard of travelling to the West of England.
Anyone having news of the above should communicate with
Sir Josh. Foulacre, c/o the *Mercury* Office.

I had scarce read the dread words when there was a
loud knockg. at the door and I seized my pistol and hid
behind the curtains. However, it proved to be merely
Roderick who came whistlg. into the room, sayg. 'Why
are you hidg. behind the curtains, Father? Are you not
rather old to be playg. hide-and-seek?' at which he
began laughing immoderately at his little jest. But I
silenced him by drawg. his attention to the newspaper
and when he had spelled out the words his face grew
pale, he breathed heavily and sat down upon the sofa
suckg. his thumb, as is his wont when troubled.

When a quart of Madeira had restored his nerves
somewhat we held a Council and agreed to leave Bath at
once. We therefore packed our scanty belongings, and
prepared to leave at dawn by the first coach, hvg. fixed
upon London as a suitable destination, since there a
man may hide with some security due to the large size

of the population, and there, too, are the greatest chances for a man to make money.

And, as Roderick said, 'In London a man may have a wench when he pleases and no one be any the wiser.'

# Chapter Five
## On the Run

*Jan. 31*: Sleet. Eph. Black d. from Bloatg. of the Bowels. Took coach at dawn and much relieved to be on the turnpike to London. Before leavg. we left a note for my cousin sayg. we had been called away, and took pains to destroy his copy of the newspaper lest he should see the advertisement and claim the reward. At Marlborough spat on a man whose appearance I did not like. Our journey was uneventful until dusk, when we reached Hounslow Heath, a few miles from London. As we were passg. a thicket a masked highwayman rode out, pointed a pair of pistols at the coachman, and shouted, 'Your money or your lives!'

We were travellg. outside the coach, and when he thrust his head inside to collect the jewels from the ladies there, I took off my boot and smote him sharply on the back of the neck with the heel, at which he collapsed. I then removed from him everythg. of value, includg. his pistols, and some money and jewellery he had stolen, and gave him five secs. to make his escape before blastg. at him as he ran half-naked across the heath. The occupants of the coach being in great admiration of my feat, Roderick took up a collection for me and raised 0£ 7s. 8³/₄d.

Arrived at an inn in London after dark. No sooner had we descended from the coach than Roderick implored me, 'Please Father, let me go and look at the women,' he hvg. heard exaggerated reports of the qualities of London females. But I forbade it, knowg. he would want to spend money on them. So we retired to bed and slept soundly after our long journey.

*Feb. 1*: Rain. A gentln. named Dr. Joseph Priestley is reported to have blown up sevl. persons at a meetg. of the Royal Society, whilst demonstratg. the properties of the Oxygen Gas. Walked the streets with Roderick in a.m. spyg. out the land. Much pleased to see such large numbers of Dissenters and foreigners etc. present, so that in one street in St. James's alone I was able to abuse three Methodists, two Quakers, a Baptist and four Frenchmen.

Dined at a coffee-house where we had a fine example of London manners, viz: upon my givg. the waiter sixpence for a cut from the joint, he held out his hand for something for himself. I declined to give him anythg. Roderick, however, said: 'I should like some gravy'. Upon which he poured a jug of gravy over Roderick's head. ITEM: To wig, 0£ 0s. 9d.; to gravy 0£ 0s. 0¼d.

In p.m. Roderick begged leave and some money to amuse himself, and capered away down the Strand whilst I sauntered about the Town observg. what might be useful, especially the location of the numerous clubs, gaming establishments and coffee-houses.

Whilst passg. an inn called the Turk's Head, in Gerrard Street, Soho, I felt hungry and went in to call for supper. The company there were v. dull, listeng.

intently to a rough, uncouth fellow with a Staffordshire accent whose name was S. Johnson, declaimg. upon life and morality without ceasg. He appeared to have a prejudice against Scotland. Upon his describg. a tour he had made of that country, I banged on the table to attract attention and animadverted as follows, viz: 'Sir, the noblest prospect that a Scotchman ever sees is the high road that leads him to England.'

At this the company laughed, except for the talkative Johnson, who said, 'Sir, you are impudent. I do not know what right you have to talk to me about Scotland.' To this I immediately replied, 'Much may be made of a Scotchman if he be caught young.' Another gentln. observed, 'You will offend Boswell's patriotism,' to which I replied with one of my wittiest sallies, viz: 'Sir, patriotism is the last refuge of a scoundrel.'

I then realised that a pallid-faced young man was writg. down my finest witticisms in a notebook. Fearg. him to be some govt. agent or possibly a Jacobite spy I seized the book from him, cast it into the fire and emptied the punch bowl over his head.

A great uproar ensued in which the fellow Johnson kept bellowg. 'Sir, you are impertinent' at the top of his voice. Fortunately another gentln. named Garrick fell down in a drunken fit. This distracted attention from me somewhat and I retired precipitately outside. As I was standg. on the pavement in front of the inn, there was a loud noise, the door opened, and a gentln. named Mr. Sheridan flew past me horizontally, hvg. been expelled for tellg. S. Johnson that he thought the visitor wittier than he.

Returned to our inn and found Roderick in bed, much distressed as he had given a girl fourpence on

Westminster Bridge thinkg. her to be a whore, only to find she was sellg. gingerbread.

*Feb. 2*: Jasper Monk overcome by fumes from the Fleet Ditch and d. instantly. Slept ill, owg. to a piece of gingerbread secreted in my night shirt. Sallied forth to a coffee-house in a.m. and read the papers. As we were doing so a great crowd of people ran by shoutg. 'Fire, fire!' A waiter informed us Dr. Joseph Priestley had been demonstratg. the properties of Phlogiston* to the Royal Society.

I told Roderick it was time we began in earnest to mend our fortunes, in pursuit of which aim we sauntered to Change Alley, where I endeavoured to sell my 200,000 shares in the South Sea Co. However, no one would buy, although a gentln. offered me five thousand shares in a company for Draining the English Channel.

Upon noticg. Roderick in conversation with a person of somewhat exuberant dress I hastened up, only to hear him say, 'Father, our fortunes are made! I have just purchased 10,000 shares in the Grand Circular Canal Co.!'

I begged of him where he had the money and he replied, 'Oh, I used two sovs. I had in my pocket left over from the money you have given me. The shares are only valued at a quarter of a groat each, as all the water keeps running out of the canal.'

---

*The Phlogiston fallacy dominated eighteenth-century science. It was wrongly believed that burning substances gave off a gas called Phlogiston, leaving a residue that was 'dephlogisticated'. The theory was exploded by Lavoisier, the great French scientist.

In p.m. went out to fulfil the greatest ambition of my life, viz: to have a shilling whore, the first time since 1745 when my father treated me to one in celebration of the defeat of The Young Pretender at Culloden. London is the only place in the kingdom where such may be obtained, as befits the greatest city in Europe.

But alas, they had all been hired by Edmund Burke for a meeting of Members of Parliament and only the twopenny ones were left, so I went away disappointed.

*Feb. 3*: Hail. The Parish Beadle of St. Marylebone is reported to have been set upon by a group of orphans who demanded more gruel and severely beat him with their spoons.

It being Sunday, in a.m. I visited the parish church and asked the Rector to say special prayers for Genl. Burgoyne and that his Stratagem of pretending to be defeated by the Pennsylvanians and Virginians will be successful.

In p.m. as I walked along a thoroughfare called Fleet Street I saw a person who by his appearance was plainly an American. I crossed the street and addressed him thus, viz: 'Vile, evil, tax-evading Bostonian, are you not ashamed of your rebellion which has brought such sorrow to his Majesty that he has gone mad and to Lord North that he has gone bald?'

Before he could reply I spat upon him, an exceptionally large expectoration, probably my best effort since I voided upon a Papist priest at the Horse Fair last Candlemas. To my dismay he raised his stick and shouted, 'Schweinhund! Donner und Blitzen but you shall suffer for this, unspeakable Englishman!'

I instantly fell to my knees in dismay and cried, 'Your

pardon sir, I did not realise you were Italian. Pray forgive me, I was overwrought.'

But my apology seemed to enrage him even further and he produced a cudgel and struck me over the head with such velocity that I was prostrated upon the pavement.

*Feb. 4*: Thunder. *The Daily Courant* prints an alarming report today, viz: that many cattle have been struck by a Lunatick Distemper. In London, a cow is said to have stood on its hind legs at Smithfield and sung 'Drink To Me Only With Thine Eyes'; while at Cambridge a Jersey heifer disputed the 39 Articles in Latin with a learned Fellow. The Archbishop of Canterbury has preached a sermon saying these omens portend some calamity and The Great Comet is about to strike the globe. May God have mercy upon us and delay this terrible happening until I can sell my shares.

*Feb. 5*: Lightning. Great Comet not landed yet. Jas. Woodhouse shot himself for no apparent reason. *The Gentleman's Magazine* says the Lunatick Distemper can infect humans and the King's madness may have been taken from a cow. When Lord North reported recently on the ingratitude of the American Colonialists, he is said to have pawed the ground and tried to butt the Minister before bursting into tears.

In p.m. a man told me that if any Lunatick Cattle are found in the locality the magistrates will commit them to Bedlam until they recover their wits.

*Feb. 6*: Wind. No sign of Great Comet. While crossing The Square I saw a vagrant called Twisted Tom being whipped at the tail of the hangman's cart. They say he did dress himself in a pair of horns and exposed himself lewdly in Fleet Street, all the time crying, 'Ho, ho, ho, I am a Lunatick Bull, ho, ho, ho.'

For fear of catching the Distemper I would eat no beef at dinner and had to content myself with a hare pie, a braised turnip and a gallon of punch with four botts. of port. The pie was bad and I do not like turnips so made do with the liquor.

Early to bed, sore hungry, but awoken just before midnight by a sound outside. On looking from the window of the inn percvd. a pair of horns waving about in the darkness, from which appeared to emanate a strange noise. 'This is Twisted Tom up to his pranks,' I thought, and seizing my largest club, the one I keep for poachers and servants, crept outside, where I raised the club and brought it down with all my force between the horns.

This had no effect so I repeated the blow when I became aware this was not Twisted Tom, but a bull which had escaped from Smithfield. I turned to flee, but lowering his head he tossed me so savagely that I landed back in the bedroom via the window, which unfortunately was not open. ITEM: Plaisters, 0£ 0s. 1¹/₂d.

*Feb. 8*: Dined at a coffee-house & asked where we might gamble in p.m. Advised to try the Cocoa Tree or Almack's and we accordingly repaired to the latter where we were soon in play with two gentln. of the highest quality, viz: Lord Sandwich and a Mr. Pitt. The stakes were a good deal higher than at Bath and bets of 10,000 sovs. were frequent, which was somewhat disconcertg. as I had only 18 sovs. on me, being all that remained of our Bath profits after we had fitted ourselves out. By good fortune I was able to increase this modest sum and becomg. emboldened increased the stakes until eventually on our opponents' wager we stood to gain or lose 5,000 sovs. Roderick and I were usg. our patent Haggard Telegraph with the backscratcher, as at Bath, but alas, Roderick became seized with a terrible itch which could only be relieved by use of the scratcher. Whilst he was doing this I mistook his action for a signal and played the wrong card.

The loss of 5,000 sovs. at one swoop left me momentarily stupified, although our opponents showed little emotion. Mr. Pitt merely remarked, 'A trifle, eh? Hardly enough to bribe a Member of Parliament these days.' Lord Sandwich grunted, 'Times are so changed, even a rascally Navy dockyard contractor would turn up his nose at a sum like that.' Then he calmly entered the sum upon a list of losgs. and winngs. Roderick however, turned pale and his teeth began to chatter to such an extent I was obliged to inform our noble opponents that he was subject to the Ague.

I said to our opponents that I was sure they would give us our revenge. To this Lord Sandwich replied, 'Damme, revenge? I hope you're not thinkg. of going yet are ye? I never quit the table until I can't see the cards, and Mr. Fox over there keeps it up for two days at a time.' With which he ordered another quart of port and we set to again.

*Feb. 9*: Rain. When dawn came we were still at play, and there were many others still at it, too. A gentln.

standg. by whispered, 'Lord Sandwich thinks nothg. of gamblg. continually for two days, win or lose.' By eight a.m. we were all feelg. hungry and Lord Sandwich called for a dish of his own invention, viz: a piece of bread is smeared with butter and a slice of meat is placed upon it, another piece of bread being placed on top. A pile of these being placed by the table, together with fresh decanters of Madeira, we entered the fray with renewed vigour, except for Roderick who kept fallg. asleep with his eyes open. Mr. Pitt, however, declined the comestibles, and ordered a veal pie from Bellamy's.

Our fortunes swayed to and fro with alarmg. rapidity. By midday I was the owner not only of 50,000 sovs., but of half Derbyshire as well, together with a seat in Parliament, five whorehouses and the town of Deal.

'I fear it is time for us to depart,' I said lookg. at Roderick and risg. from the table.

'I think not,' said Lord Sandwich as he shuffled the cards. 'We have hardly begun yet. I'm sure a sportg. gentln. like yourself wouldn't deprive us of the chance of revenge.'

He smiled grimly as he spoke, with an expression not unlike the grin of a large snake, so I hastily sat down and remarked, 'It is a matter of total indifference to myself.' With which I promptly lost 3,000 sovs. and when a dish of tea was served later I had lost all my winngs. In addition I owed Lord Sandwich 35,000 sovs., Haggard Hall, all my worldly goods and the sixpence which Roderick keeps round his neck.

*Feb. 10*: Midnight struck but still the battle continued as Dame Fortune cast her favours wildly, first one side and now the other, the players stoppg. only to consume large quantities of my Lord Sandwich's Patent Comestibles, until four o'clock the next morning when My Lord flung down his cards, and cried, 'Damme, I've had enough, I've got to go huntg. in three hours' time.'

By this time our debts were reduced to a mere half-sov.; and grateful I was to escape with such small loss. Although our profits at Bath had given Roderick and I enough money for a short time, economy was still important. So I deemed it prudent to pay Lord Sandwich with a counterfeit half-sov. given to me by Wat Blast for some sheep I sold him. All would have been well had not his Lordship been so fuddled with fatigue and wine that he dropped the coin as I gave it to him. It struck the floor with a dull thud, much unlike the ring of true coin, also being found to be bent when he picked it up.

After peerg. closely at the coin, Lord Sandwich bit it, and it immediately fell in half. He then handed me the pieces with the followg. remark, viz: 'Sir, you are a d—d cheat, a forger and a scoundrel and I hope it will not be necessary for me to strike you before you give me the satisfaction that is my due.'

I replied no man had ever called a Haggard those names and lived. 'There is a good explanation but I do not deign to give it.' I declared. 'Let your seconds wait upon me tomorrow' (thinkg. I can flee the city before they arrive). Lord Sandwich, however, said drily, 'I don't doubt you would prefer to wait until tomorrow, when doubtless you will have been called away urgently.' He preferred to meet upon the instant and would provide attendants to escort me to the proper place for such a meetg. With which four large footmen entered and forcibly conveyed myself and Roderick into a coach and away to a lonely field near Kensington Village.

Roderick wailed for mercy until he discovered he did not have to fight, upon which he was all for 'showg. My Lord a taste of gunpowder' and suchlike sentiments; which he could well afford to make, not hvg. to risk his life.

Upon arrival at the field Lord Sandwich's second, the gentln. named Pitt, produced a case of pistols, but I said I would use my own. I therefore took out the horse-pistol I had taken from the highwayman near Hounslow, and charged it with a handsome portion of old nails. By now there were a dozen other persons present, includg. a chirurgeon, an undertaker and sevl. gentln. from Almack's.

It was agreed Mr. Pitt should start the duel by droppg. a handkerchief as a signal to open fire; we took the regulation number of paces and turned round to face each other. My emotions were those of the strongest terror; indeed, I would have called out an apology if I thought it would have been accepted. I glanced at Roderick for support, but he had turned away and stuffed his fingers in his ears against the noise of the pistols.

The field of fire from my horse-pistol being so wide I had little need to take careful aim. Instead I concentrated upon the handkerchief in the starter's hand. The instant it began to fall I shouted loudly, 'Look behind you, My Lord, for G—'s sake,' and then fired my charge.

Hvg. inserted a double amount of powder to make sure of a powerful blast I was thrown on to my back by the velocity of the explosion, but when the smoke cleared I percvd. all the spectators lying on the ground riddled with old nails and exhibitg. tokens of the deepest distress. My Lord Sandwich alone remained erect, dazed by the shock of the explosion and starg. wildly about him. His pistol, however, was still smokg. from which I deduced that the vibration of my charge had caused him to fire inadvertently. Before he could reload, I ran up and struck him violently upon the top of his head with the butt-end of my weapon, upon which he gave a feeble groan and collapsed insensible upon the grass.

I then turned to Roderick. He lay moang. gently and his breeches riddled with holes, but I soon discovered that mercifully his injuries were but slight, as were those of the other onlookers, who were all conveyed to a nearby Spital. So was My Lord, still insensible. Roderick I took back to our inn myself, where we bathed his wounds in brandy.

*Editor's Note: Despite every endeavour no reference to this duel can be found in the private papers of Lord Sandwich. But it is certain that Haggard had no doubts that he had fought Lord Sandwich to the day he died, and Roderick too believed the same, for in later years he would try to impress women by showing them a rusty nail 'Which I recvd. in the rear durg. the great duel between my Father and Lord Sandwich.' Those women with whom he had an intimate relationship would be shown the actual wound. Further evidence comes from the house-keeper's accounts at Haggard Hall a year or two later, which contain frequent references to 'meat and bread for the Sandwiches' at a time when the newly-invented dish had not yet won wide popularity.*

For the remainder of the day we rested, Roderick lying face downwards on the bed whilst I sponged his rear with a soothg. lotion at regular intervals. ITEM: To soothg. lotion for the Injured Seat 0£ 0s. 1³/₄d.

*Feb. 11*: Hail. His Majesty the King reported to have bitten Lord North. No news of General Burgoyne today. I slept late and was awoken by the sound of a distant explosion. Upon enquirg. from a servant girl the occasion she replied, 'People say, sir, it is that there Dr. Joseph Priestley inventg. hydrochloric acid.' Perused newspapers in coffee-house in a.m. Was alarmed to see a reference to the duel in the followg. terms, viz:

> We understand there was an affray of honour at Kensington early yesterday involvg. a certain noble Lord and a gentln. from the country named Haggard, and that My Noble Lord came off worst in the encounter, being confined to his bed with a wound in the head which is not serious. Perhaps this wound will allow the escape of certain Heady Vapours from which My Lord has been sufferg. recently.

This threw me into not a little confusion, lest the report should give away our whereabouts to either Sir Josh. or the Bailiffs. However, there was little we could do about it. Upon readg. further I percvd. an advertisement for a Boxing Match that afternoon in Parliament Hill Fields for fifty guineas a side between Jas. Turnip, of Peckham, and Wm. Thrasher, of Godalming. Roderick and I accordingly travelled there in the hope that we might win some money by wagers.

A large crowd was gathered and money was being

placed freely on both contenders at roughly equal odds. I therefore told Roderick to move amongst the crowd spreadg. a rumour that Jas. Turnip had sprained his wrist, and when the odds against him began to lengthen I laid large sums of money upon him. I then myself moved amongst the crowd whisperg., 'They say that Wm. Thrasher hurt his ankle jumpg. from a coach, and yesterday he could hardly stand up.' When the odds against him duly lengthened Roderick wagered an equally large sum upon the said Wm. Thrasher.

Thus being assured of winng. whatever the result, we watched the bout with equanimity. Alas, Fate dashed our hopes for, in the 99th round, after the fight had gone on for five hours, Wm. Thrasher collapsed on top of Jas. Turnip and both fell to the ground insensible. Supporters of each man instantly rushed into the ring and began to kick them in an effort to make them get up, but all to no avail and the fight was abandoned as a draw, so we won nothg. Worse, when we went to collect our bets, the fellow who had taken them had ran off.

Supped at an inn upon a boiled sheep's head which made Roderick sick. Took a boat to Ranelagh Gardens and won 17 sovs. at gamblg. which helped repair the day's losses. Roderick's injuries much better.

*Feb. 12*: When we were breakfastg. at the inn the Boots told us some persons had been enquirg. for us the previous day. I became apprehensive and asked who they were.

'The first two looked like Law Officers' he said, 'and the other was a person of quality, one Sir. Josh. Foulacre.'

At the sound of that dreadful name my heart sank

and Roderick turned white. 'Sir Josh. Foulacre!' I ejaculated. 'How did he know we were here?'

'He said he was in London on some affairs, sir, saw a report concerng. you in the newspaper and made enquiries. Is he a relative of yours, sir? He seemed most anxious to see you again.'

At this I tarried no longer but hurried Roderick to our room, packed our chest and decamped into the street there and then, without payg. the reckoning. I then dragged Roderick (and our chest) into a coffee-house to discuss what to do. We dare not stay in London with Sir Josh. and the law officers knowg. our whereabouts; even now they might be scourg. the coffee-houses and inns.

Roderick began to snivel. 'Nowhere in England is safe,' he wailed. 'We shall be hounded and persecuted throughout the land.' I declared he was right: we must undertake the Grand Tour of Europe, where nobody knew us. Roderick objected again, and said, 'We shall be murdered or poisoned or die in a Plague or perhaps all three.' But I soothed him by describg. the unusual Pleasures of Venus of which we might partake and how it was certain he could make an advantageous and wealthy match in Europe, where princesses were two-a-penny and Englishmen highly regarded.

'Remember,' I told him, 'that he who now sits upon the Throne of England is but the descendant of a German Prince.'

'Aye,' replied Roderick sulkily, 'and he's mad as a hatter too, as everyone well knows, and his son is poxed up to the eyebrows, even though he's only seventeen.' Notwithstandg. his objections I persuaded him to agree

79

and we lay hidden all day to await the first coach of the day to Dover at dawn.

# Chapter Six
## Paris Interlude

*Feb. 13*: I thought it unlikely the Dover coach would be watched, nevertheless deemed it prudent to send Roderick ahead to see. He reported all was clear, and with our faces muffled up so as not to be recognised, we took the coach, sittg. inside. A weary journey, made worse by a d—d cantg. clergyman who told us lies of a fantastickal nature, viz: that a sailor named Cook had discovered a new continent in the Antipodes, when it is well-known that the region is inhabited by giants with their heads beneath their shoulders.

However, the further we were removed from London, the merrier became my spirits. By Canterbury I was sufficiently recovered to give my celebrated impersonation of the Archbishop of Canterbury deliverg. a sermon whilst intoxicated. This jovial jest kept both myself and Roderick happy, although the clergyman was not amused.

It being too late to take passage to France that night, we put up at an inn, and found the inn and the town so d—d dull that I was reduced to attemptg. to debauch the chambermaid. As she resisted so little I abandoned the effort.

*Feb. 14*: Gales. Jonas Forge hanged for drillg. a hole in the bottom of the Excise Cutter. After breakfast we enquired for the Calais Packet, and took ship with a motley collection which included sevl. Frenchmen.

No sooner had we left the shelter of the harbour than the motion of the waves became v. violent and Roderick was heartily sea-sick. His suffergs. were so great that he begged, 'Kill me, Father. I do not wish to live,' and indeed, feebly pawed at his pocket in an effort to remove his penknife and cut his own throat.

Percvg. that Nature was about to prove too strong for Roderick, I cried, 'Not towards me dear boy, face towards that group of French priests,' and so sayg. I turned him so that he voided his stomach over the Miserable Romans as they were kneelg. in the middle of their superstitious practices.

The shore of France was eventually reached after several hours and we entered Calais, and Roderick and I were at last beyond the reach of the English Law and Sir Josh., although in poor condition otherwise, havg. little but our wits and a few score pounds between us and destitution.

Upon arrival in the loathsome land of Toads and Pederasts I went ashore immediately, dragging Roderick behind me and treadg. on some people kneelg. on the quay and givg. thanks for preservation in their outlandish tongue.

Handg. a child a groat to carry our chest, I marched to an inn, seized the innkeeper by the throat, and told him, 'Hey there, M. Crapaud, know you that an English Milord and his son have arrived, so prepare your best room *tout suite*.' He made no reply, and I was about to strike him when I realised I was still holdg. him by his Norman throat. Upon being released he led us upstairs to a miserable room which he indicated was the best in the house.

I demanded Port, Madeira and Canary, but in vain. All the landlord could produce was a glass of local wine of such sour quality that I threw it at him and demanded brandy, which I consumed in copious quantities. Roderick being unable to eat I dined late and alone upon the smallest chicken I have ever seen in my life. Upon percvg. the size of the bird I remarked, 'If it were any smaller it would be an egg,' but the landlord feigned not to understand my witticism, it being well-known that the Gallic character lacks any distinction of what is amusg., unlike the wholesome English temperament.

After dinner I went about the town insulting Frenchmen, of which there were an unusually large number, but as some insulted me back I was compelled to desist. After I had kicked a particularly large Papist, a person standg. near said he presumed from my behaviour I was an English gentln. Upon my signifyg. this was so he said that he, too, had just arrived from England and asked me to join him in a glass. We went to an inn. After some conversation he asked what part of England I came from and then remarked, 'I wonder if you know a particular friend of mine, good old Sir Josh. Foulacre? There is a fine old English gentln. for you.'

My agitation at this was so great that I spilled my drink, regained my composure however, and said I had heard of Sir Josh. and asked where he was at that moment, fearg. he had come to France. The stranger said Sir Josh. had been in Bath, where he had slain two footpads who attempted to garrotte him in a dark alley one night. He was now in London.

'Sir Josh.,' said the stranger, 'went to Bath to seek out some people who had insulted his daughter. He had apparently challenged them to a duel but they fled. However, they will not escape. He is a man utterly devoted to the task in hand. He will seek them out wherever they are and I would not like to be in their shoes when he finds them.'

At this I made some excuse and hastily took my leave, returng. to our inn where I drank a jug of wine before I was restored.

*Feb. 15*: Fog. King Louis XVI reported to have thrown a commode cabinet at Jean-Jacques Rousseau. Whilst walkg. along the high road a peasant named Hippolyte was driven down by an aristocrat, and d. instantly. We lingered no longer in a.m. than necessary. Upon the landlord presentg. us with a reckong. for some 5 *livres* I tore it up and gave him a few small coins, tellg. him he should have been honoured to have had as his guest an English Milord and his son. So we left Calais with his Gallic curses about our ears in the coach.

I make it an infallible rule when travellg. abroad to see as little of the scenery as possible; thus the mind is not unsettled and disturbed by wild excesses of Nature and barren deserts such as the Scottish Highlands. My invariable custom is to attempt to drink a bott. of port for each league travelled and this custom I continued this day, albeit hvg. to substitute brandy for port; I therefore have no recollection of the journey to Paris except for the first few miles, when I was v. impressed with the subservience of the peasantry, who cringed when an aristocrat rode past.

As an experiment I spat on one and he made no reply, where your sturdy English labourer would have cried 'D— you for a d—d landowner' and spat back, unless he had been a Quaker, when he wd. have revenged himself by stealth.

*Editor's Note: Haggard's custom of drinking himself into oblivion seems only too habitual. This is the sole memorandum we have of the three-day journey to Paris, a city which he seems to have entered in a state of intoxication, as the next entry is dated three days later, the day after he entered the city.*

*Feb. 18*: Rain. Upon arisg. we percvd. a dense cloud of smoke over the city and were informed the celebrated M. Lavoisier had blown up the University in tryg. to split water into Hydrogen and Oxygen. In a.m. visited the principal sights of the city with Roderick. Saw the leadg. gaols, dungeons, places of execution, charnel houses, & etc. & etc. Was v. impressed by an especially large House of Correction called the Bastille, which contained many dungeons, and I made a short sketch of this interestg. buildg. with a view to erectg. a smaller copy in England, should we be preserved to set foot on our native soil again.

*Editor's Note: Haggard's sketch of his proposed English Bastille is still preserved in the Muniment Room at Haggard Hall. It was never built.*

I deemed it a worthwhile stratagem to disguise our names whilst in Paris, both for secrecy and with the intention of imposg. upon the French, such is the

power of the aristocratic name here. I therefore adopted
the pseudonym of Viscount Birmingham; Roderick
became the Hon. Roderick. Ordered some beef to be
dressed for dinner; as it was neither roasted nor boiled,
but prepared in some weird French way, we threw it out
of the window and hit an aristocrat on the head.

Visited a tailor's shop and ordered two suits of
clothes, the tailor promisg. us he would make them
suitable for a pair of English Milords. Spent p.m. tryg.
to make wagers with Frenchmen, but they are such
poor sportsmen no one would wager with us.


*Feb. 19*: Rain. Plague raging in Cadiz. Jacques le
Brun d. from les Emissions Vertes. Up early and to the
tailor's, where we put on our new suits. These have
been made in a fantastickal manner, the French idea of
what an English Milord would wear. Thus there is so
much lace on the cuffs that I have to hold my hands in
the air or else I trip over it, whilst the tails of Roderick's
coat are so long he keeps treadg. on them. Both of us
have coats and waistcoats of mauve, trimmed with gold,
whilst our breeches are orange.

Afterwards, we swaggered about the City, much
admired in our new clothes. Roderick pranced wildly
through the streets actg. as he imagined an English
Milord wd. behave in Paris. He cried continually,
'Faugh! Damme! Stap me vitals but these Froggies are a
d—d peculiar bunch,' and consumed snuff in great
handfuls, so that within a few mins. he was quite brown
about the face and had to be washed in a fountain. A
small crowd was attracted by his antics and began to
follow us about the streets, tappg. their foreheads, so I
counselled him, 'Restrain your Thespian ardour, my

son. You look like Garrick performg. Richard III when drunk, and that was frequent enough, G— knows. Save the play-actg. for an occasion when it will profit us, as to impress some wealthy young woman.'

We called upon the English Consul, who said there was a ball that eveng. at the house of the Duc de Camembert, and he knew we should be welcome if he mentioned it to the Duke, which we desired him to do. Ate a chicken fricassee for dinner and some cheese, but the cheese being bad in one particular, viz: it was full of large holes, we refused to pay for it.

In p.m. attended the ball given by the Duc de Camembert at a fashionable house near the Tuileries. I told Roderick, 'Lose no opportunity to make a profitable alliance, for even a French girl of noble birth is better than nothg. As for me, I intend to gamble the night away. And above all, be careful.'

The Duke welcomed us warmly, together with the Consul. He also introduced us to the Duchess, a comely woman of thirty-five. I left Roderick talkg. to them whilst I made my excuses and joined some persons playg. vingt-et-un and piquet. I had soon won 20 *Louis d'or* and looked around for Roderick but was unable to perceive him. At that moment my attention was distracted by a gentln. called the Marquis de Lafayette, who commenced a tirade in favour of the American Colonialists, as a result of which the followg. dialogue ensued, viz:

MARQUIS DE LAFAYETTE: Believe me, Monsieur, Gen. Burgoyne is completely defeated. He is fleeg. in disorder. He may have surrendered already.

SELF: Permit me to correct you in one particular,

Monsieur. Gen. Burgoyne is not retreatg., he is takg. up winter quarters.

MARQUIS: Ha, ha, ha. Allow me to inform you, Monsieur, that the Americans have him by the tail and will not let him go.

SELF: Allow me to inform you, Monsieur, that you are a stupid Gallic Worm.

MARQUIS: Permit me to transmit the intelligence that you are a perfidious English Pig.

SELF: Pray do me the honour, sir, of leapg. into the most proximate heap of manure.

MARQUIS: I would be vastly obliged if you would do me the service of jumpg. into the Seine, fully-clothed.

Our discussion lasted almost an hour and was not terminated until I thrust the Frenchman's head into a fruit tart.

There was still no sign of Roderick. My trepidation knew no bounds when I discovered the beautiful Duchess had also disappeared, although the Duke was still present. Makg. some excuse I left the table and searched the house for my son. I was convinced he had given way to that Fatal Amorous Impetuosity of the Haggards, and was languishing with the Duchess in the Rites of Aphrodite, a connection which could only end in disaster for us both, knowg. the jealous Gallic temperament.

For an hour I searched the huge house, every moment expect. to hear a shot or shriek which would announce the discovery of the lovers. Weary of my fruitless search I began to look round the garden. For some minutes I searched in vain; then my attention was drawn by the violent agitation of some shrubbery. I hastened to the spot and partg. the bushes found to my inexpressible horror Roderick and the Duchess de Camembert locked in an embrace and indulgg. in the tenderest offices of Venus. Such was their passion that they failed to hear my approach or expostulations of warng.

I was about to kick Roderick when there was a disturbance in the undergrowth and the Duke arrived with ten servants carryg. muskets and torches. He took in the situation at a glance and nodded at the men, who seized the unhappy couple and tore them apart savagely. Realisg. what had happened Roderick began to blubber for mercy and fell on his knees. I added my own pleas, tellg. the Duke, 'Fear not sir, this is but an English custom and intended as a tribute to the host rather than otherwise.'

The Duke answered but one word: 'Merde'. He then seized a loaded musket from one of his servants, advanced upon Roderick, halted a few feet away and pointed the muzzle at those parts of the Human Anatomy Sacred to the Offices of Venus. Words cannot express my horror when I saw his foul intention, an action only a Gallic Toad would be capable of. The Duchess shrieked with terror, and flung herself at the Duke's feet, but was dragged away. Roderick remained as if turned to stone, his face as white as chalk, whilst I was rooted to the spot with apprehension.

Raisg. the musket to his shoulder, the Duke took careful aim at Roderick's loins, the muzzle of the gun being a mere yard from its delicate target, and slowly squeezed the trigger. 'Die, seducg. English pig!' he cried and fired. There was a vivid flash, a loud bang and a cloud of smoke. The Duchess screamed whilst poor Roderick let out the most terrible screech ever uttered by human voice. The violence of the explosion flung him backwards to the ground, where he lay prostrate as midnight struck from a nearby church.

*Feb. 20*: Drizzle. Duc d'Orleans excommunicated again. Upon percvg. Roderick lying without signs of animation on the ground I shouted, 'You shall pay for this, Frog-eating Monsieur Crapaud!' and ran to my son.

There was no outward sign of injury, except a scorch-mark on his breeches from the nearness of the explosion, and I was about to undress him when I percvd. the Duke was examing. the muzzle of his musket. Suddenly with a cry of 'Mon Dieu!'* he hurled the gun at one of the servants and shouted, 'Cochon!†　You have forgotten to put a bullet in it! Nom d'un Chien!‡ Give me another and make sure it is loaded this time, insufferable imbecile!'§

Realisg. what had happened I took advantage of the confusion, seized a stick from the ground and pointed it at the Duke with a shout of, 'Stand back you pack of Frog rascals! The first man who stirs dies by my hand!', hopg. that in the dim light of the torches, the branch would be mistaken for a pistol. My ruse worked, and the French held back for a moment.

Durg. this brief respite Roderick, who was weakly stirrg., came to his senses and sat up. Immediately, I slapped his face to revive him and told him: 'Run for your life!' Fortunately he regained his wits with a great

* 'My God!'　　　†'Pig!'　　‡'Name of a dog!'　　§'Imbecile!'

start and shot off through the bushes with such velocity I could hardly keep up. Within seconds we were fleeg. through the garden, aided on our way by a blast from the Duke.

On my earlier perambulations I had gained some idea of the arrangement of the gardens and percvd. that the Duke and his servants were between us and the principal gate, for which they would believe me to make. I therefore hurried Roderick in the other direction, hopg. we might find another entrance or scale the wall.

We soon reached the wall, only to find it ten feet high and with no signs of any aperture. We hastily searched its length and then heard the sounds of pursuit approachg. There was no time for further delay. I bent down and told Roderick, 'Climb on my back and gain the top. Hasten!' This he did with such celerity that he vanished clean over the top and down the other side before I could instruct him to wait and pull me up.

I shouted over the wall, 'You are a d—d fool and how do you think I can get over?' To which he replied he had not thought of that. 'Perhaps you can escape by disguisg. yourself as a Frenchman and walkg. through the main gate?' he called out. There was no time to upbraid him. I could see the torches of the servants little more than a hundred yards away, and hear the Duke shoutg., 'A thousand *Louis* for the man who secures them!' Telling Roderick to remain where he was I ran along the foot of the wall, seekg. some openg. or opportunity to scale it.

A tree growg. near seemed to offer the best chance and I had just jumped up and seized one of the lower branches when I heard a shout of, 'Il est là!

Tirez, tirez!'* There came the sound of an explosion and bullets whistled about my person. Fear, like Love, can inspire men to the impossible and with a great heave I pulled myself up on to the branch, crawled along it, and leaped the gap between it and the wall.

For a moment I hung by my fingers, but was able to scrabble to the top where I lay pantg. before slidg. down into the street, where Roderick was waitg. We immediately took to our heels and did not stop until we were safe at our inn.

*Feb. 23*:  Bishop of Rheims poisoned by Lutherans. For three days Roderick has been forced to keep to his bed, attended by d—d French doctors who insist upon payment before attendance and then say they can do nothg. He has no physical hurts, but is sorely distressed. He whines continually and has scarcely slept since the affair, wakg. up in the night and cryg. 'Mercy! Do not fire!' and continually examing. his Nether Parts for signs of injury.

Today Roderick arose in a.m. and appeared a little better. Visited by the British Consul, who expressed alarm at Roderick's behaviour.

'I would suggest that you leave Paris at once,' he told us, 'or else I will not be answerable for your safety. Because of the conflict in America, Englishmen are hardly popular here in any case.'

I asserted nothg. would give me greater pleasure than to leave this Haunt of Garlic-Smellg., Jabberg. Cuckolds, provided the Consul would supply us with money to reach Germany, where we were certain to

---

* 'There he is! Fire, fire!'

recover our fortunes. The Consul said he could not do this, but there was an Englishman leavg. that day in a coach for Venice, and he would doubtless be pleased to offer us free passage in return for the protection and pleasure of our company. The Consul would press the matter.

Our desire to leave Paris was so great we assented immediately and agreed to meet the gentln. in the afternoon. Spent rest of day inside the inn for fear of further revenges by the Duke, until the hour of our departure when I sallied forth with Roderick and a French boy carryg. our little luggage, followed by the curses of the landlord's wife, a vile crone named Madame Defarge who spends most of her time knitting.

She swore she had never yet been paid her full score by a 'cursed aristo' and shouted after us, 'You may laugh now, but you will all pay for this in ten years' time, aye you and every cursed single one of the aristos! You will all hang from the lamp-posts!' To which I retorted, 'I hope, Madam, that you will have the goodness to put out the light first,' and hurried away.

The coach was waitg. when we arrived at the rendez-vous and met our travellg. companion, who turned out to be none other than our acquaintance from Bath, the Hon. Cholmondley-Fitzroy! Our surprise was mutual. The Hon. greeted us warmly, cryg. out, 'Haw, haw, haw, but damme if it isn't that young Haggard and his sire, damme, haw, haw, haw, pleased to meet you again, don't you know?'

We asked why he had left England and he said he was undertakg. the Grand Tour at short notice owg. to an Unpleasant Occurence in Bath.

'I was hoppg. round the Assembly Rooms on one leg,

for a wager of 200£, with one of me friends,' the Hon. C-F explained, 'when I accidentally hopped on to the toe of a fellow named Sir Josh. Foulacre. Well it must have hurt the fellow a good deal, 'cos it was his gouty foot, don't you know, but before I could apologise he'd seized me by the throat and challenged me to a duel. Well, haw, haw, haw, fightin' ain't in my line, don't you know, so I left Bath within the hour for London, and came on to Paris.'

His amazement knew no bounds when we told him we too, were victims of Sir Josh. 'Haw, haw, haw, but the man is as dangerous as a mad dog,' he declared.

Our intercourse was so pleasant and animated that I forgot my rule when travellg. abroad to be utterly Intoxicated most of the time, and we spent the hours makg. wagers, as a result of which I won the followg. sums, viz: As To Whom Could Expectorate Upon The Most Peasants – 5 sovs.; As To When The Next Horse Would Fart – 10 sovs.; As To Whom Could Hit A Distant House With A Pistol Shot – 15 sovs.; The Hon. C-F won a wager as To Whom Could Pull The Funniest Face (half a guinea); and Roderick won the wager as To Whom Could Put Out His Tongue The Farthest (one penny).

*Editor's Note: After this brief interlude Squire Haggard seems to have returned to his former habit of total and continual intoxication when travelling abroad. The next entry is much later.*

# Chapter Seven
## Roderick's Disaster

*March 10*: Snow. Drove over an unusually large goat-herd in a.m. As I was unable to procure sufficient brandy yesterday I was forced to remain conscious for part of the journey. We have for some days now been travellg. through a mountainous region covered in snow. I tested the depth at the side of the road by thrustg. a peasant into it, and it measured five feet. The Hon. C-F, who is learned in these matters, informs us that we are now in that country of perfumed gigolos and macaroni-eatg. Savages, viz: Italy (the part under the rule of the Kingdom of Sardinia).

Midway through dinner the coachman told us a wheel on the coach was broken and we would not be able to set off until morning. I decided to spend the time writg. up my Journal whilst Roderick and the Hon. C-F took a fowlg.-piece to see what game they could find in the hills at the back of the inn.

The pair had not returned by supper-time, although despite the darkness I did not worry, as I thought that perhaps they had found an unexpected opportunity to sample the Joys of some rural Aphrodite in a remote cottage. I accordingly ordered supper. An omelette arrived, together with some tubes of white substance.

This provg. inedible I amused myself by throwg. handfuls at the innkeeper as he went about his business.

I was constrained to drink sevl. jugs of Italian red wine which I improved by stirrg. in a few drops of cordials from my private store. The mixture proved so potent that after only four or five jugs I fell asleep with my head on the table, worn out by the fatigues of travellg. and writg. my Journal.

*March 11*: Snow. Awoke with a start from my slumber to find it was two o'clock and still no sign of the Hon. C-F and Roderick. Roused the landlord and mimed fears that something had happened to them. He returned my mime with gestures indicative of persons being crushed in an avalanche or hvg. their throats cut. I went to the door with the intention of searchg. for the lost pair but it was snowg. so hard I could scarce see six feet, so returned to bed.

Arose early and called coachman in order to conduct a search. Proposed to take the landlord with a small barrel of brandy slung round his neck to revive the lost couple. But our preparations were interrupted by the arrival of a snivellg. peasant, who said a person of strange appearance had given him a note to take to us on pain of death. I opened the note and observed it was headed with a skull and crossbones and read as follows, viz:

*To the Rich English Milord*
BRING 50,000 GOLD *PISTOLES* TO THE CROSS AT THE FOOT OF THE MOUNTAIN OR YOUR SON AND HIS FRIEND WILL DIE.

This missive was signed with a representation of a

heart pierced by a dagger.

Upon observg. the note the landlord turned pale and when he saw the sign at the end began to jabber and cross himself. I asked the coachman 'Is this some jest?' After conversation with the landlord the coachman informed me that the sign of heart and dagger was the signature of the dreaded Il Morte, leader of a terrible *Camarilla* of *Banditti* which terrorised the district.

In a show of defiance, I said to the coachman: 'Tell the landlord, and indeed any other craven-hearted Worms, to take note that I, Amos Haggard, English- man, defy the dreaded Il Morte, and tear his note into little pieces, and in any case I have not got 50,000 pence let alone 50,000 *pistoles*' with which rash statement I drank myself into insensibility.

*March 12*:  Snow. A cowherd named Garabaldi fell over a precipice and d. instantly. Awoken by the landlord, who approached with a parcel he said had just been left at the door by a terrible person with eight knives in his belt. I tore open the packet and found it contained Roderick's hair. A note said that all Englishmen were rich and if the ransom were not paid his nails would follow next day, and the rest of him piece by piece until the money was handed over, after which the Hon. C-F would follow, little by little as it were.

Upon receivg. this information I was about to drink myself into insensibility again, since I had not got the money, when a Device occured to me and I went up- stairs to our chest. After searchg. for some minutes found Roderick's 10,000 shares in the Grand Circular Canal Co. I gathered some of them together and wrote a note sayg. as follows, viz:

My dear Morte,

It is indeed true that all Englishmen are rich. But it is equally true that they never use money, since the mere word of an Englishman is worth any amount of foreign gold. I am therefore presentg. you with somethg. far more precious than 50,000 *pistoles*, viz: bonds worth thousands of pounds, not in the miserable currency of your own country but in good, English promises.

Yr. Obedient Servnt.<br>Amos Haggard, Gent

I folded the shares into a parcel, told the coachman to deliver them at the cross at the foot of the mountain, and proceeded to drink myself into a stupor, since I had done all that human hand could do, nay more.

Was aroused some hours later by voices outside and the coachman arrived with Roderick and the Hon. C–F, who upon receipt of the letter had been immediately released by the simple *Banditti*. At first I did not recognise Roderick, as all his hair had been shaved off and he had no wig. I assumed that the coachman had brought along some local buffoon to entertain me, but suddenly the bald figure let out a familiar wail and I knew it to be my dear son.

The Hon. C–F shook my hand warmly and said, 'Haw, haw, haw, it was a deuced decent thing to do, to spend your fortune on us as a ransom.'

I enquired what fortune and he said, 'Why, the 50,000 gold *pistoles* they demanded, haw, haw, haw, don't you know?'

At this I burst out laughing and replied, 'Did you not know I sent the *Banditti* 5,000 shares in the Grand Circular Canal Co.?'

For a moment they remained speechless and then both fell to the floor insensible at the shock of this discovery.

When they had recovered we celebrated their escape with a large supper and drank confusion to Il Morte. Roderick kept askg. what would have happened if Il Morte had discovered the ransom to be worthless? I privily thought he would probably have sent me Roderick's head in a parcel, but kept my thoughts to myself and merely replied that we should make an early start next day in case Il Morte changed his mind.

*March 13*: Blizzards. Left early and travelled as quickly as possible to get away from danger. The landlord followed us a little way complaing. about money we owed him until he fell into a snowdrift and was seen no more.

We had travelled about a league and were passg. down the side of a steep mountain when fifty armed *Banditti* suddenly leaped out of a cave and surrounded the coach before we could use our pistols. Roderick immediately fell to the floor of the coach whing. for mercy whilst the Hon. C–F got under the seat. Then the door was flung open by a large, fat personage wearg. a handkerchief round his head and five pistols round his waist, from whose peremptory manner I deduced to be Il Morte himself.

To my surprise he addressed me in tolerable English, viz: 'We spik about da ransom, ha?' I instantly reached in my pocket and pullg. out a few *livres* begged him to take all our gold and spare our lives, upon which he contemptuously threw the gold coins into the snow and shouted loudly, 'I no wanta da gold. I wanta more of that-a special Inglese money you send-a me yesterday.' With this he seized me by the cravat and put his knife to my throat.

For a moment sentiments of the greatest agitation flowed through my frame, until I realised what had happened, viz: the poor fool had indeed been deceived by the simple ruse and wished for more shares in the Grand Circular Canal Company. Without more ado I tore open our travellg. chest, and handed him a further 5,000 which he clutched greedily, grinng. with pleasure. When the wind blew some of them from his grasp, other members of the band surged about him and actually struggled to secure shares for themselves, cryg. 'Viva Il Grand Circular Canal Co!' and similar sentiments, while two of them fought a duel with knives over one worthless share.

So we left them wavg. their useless pieces of paper just as if they had been stockjobbers, and doubtless they were no more dishonest, with which Philosophical Reflection the coach gathered speed and we saw them no more. The Hon. C–F soon came out from under the seat but Roderick could only be restored to full use of his senses, such as they are, by the application of a large lump of snow down the back of his neck.

*March 25*: Rain. This day we at last arrived in Venice, the final stage of our journey being by boat across to the city, which appears to be a d—d damp, unhealthy place, full of foreigners and without a single proper street in the place, so that we had to be rowed to our albergo by a native of these parts called a gondolier. Upon arrival at our inn the gondolier demanded five sous. I offered three and when he protested kicked him into the canal, the waters of which were so muddy that he failed to sink and remained screamg. abuse.

When we had settled at our inn and were washg. away

the dust of the journey with some wine, the Hon. C–F addressed me as follows, viz: 'Haw, haw, haw, sir, I believe I am indebted to you for my life – no sir, do not deny it – haw, haw, haw, I believe I would have been d—d well cut into pieces by those infernal creatures if you had not ransomed me by your ingenious Stratagem. I shall be eternally grateful sir, and – haw, haw, haw – in token of my gratitude would like you to name any favour it is in my power to dispose.' He then sat back after what I believe to have been the longest speech of his life.

I instantly replied, 'You are too kind sir and I would be vastly obliged if you would lend me a thousand pounds.'

He appeared taken aback a little at this, as well he might, since he had doubtless been thinkg. I would beg of him some trumpery favour such as an introduction to the Ambassador. However, he recovered well and said, 'I shall be honoured to be of service in that way, haw, haw, haw.' Whereupon he called for pen and ink and there and then wrote out a draft for the sum upon his father's bank in London.

Words failed me as I seized the sacred document and pressed it to my bosom. I did not like to show too much pleasure in front of our benefactor, but when he had left the room I cried to Roderick, 'Our troubles are this time surely at an end! With this money we may travel as far as we like until our fortunes are made!'

Roderick feared we had asked too much, but I told him the Hon. C–F had revealed durg. the journey that his father had placed 10,000£ at his disposal, and as I said, 'Ten per centum is a small price to pay for one's life.'

I invited the Hon. C–F to be my guest at dinner and

we had a right royal feast. Our toasts included 'Damnation to the French' and 'Perish All Foreign Toads'. Roderick begged leave to introduce another and gave us '*Mort* to Il Morte', at which witticism the Hon. C-F laughed so much his chair broke. For some time we sat around the table and amused ourselves by hurlg. fruit at passg. waiters and when that paled I was about to suggest some merry wagers when the Hon. C-F slid under the table.

Roderick then begged me to give him money for a wench, as he had heard the ladies of Venice are renowned for the Generosity and Peculiarity of their Favours. I accordingly gave him a gold piece and cautioned him to be on his guard as the ladies of Venice are also renowned for the Prevalence of the Pox. He seized the coin in his hand and danced away. As for myself, I decided not to stir, but to spend the rest of the day thinkg. about money which I accordingly did with great satisfaction. Whilst musg. thus I fell asleep at the table, and was awakened shortly afterwards by a loud commotion outside the inn. I went to the door and percvd. Roderick cowerg. against the wall whilst a woman rained blows and abuse on him, callg. him 'Bambino! debole! ladre!'* and other similar epithets.

I asked Roderick what the matter was and he appeared reluctant to tell me. I commanded the wench to be quiet but she continued to scream at Roderick. Eventually I was forced to silence her by givg. her money.

Roderick hvg. been restored with some brandy I again asked him what had happened; he blushed and said, ''Twas nothg., could not a gentln. have a row with

* 'Child! idiot! thief!'

a whore without the whole world pesterg. him with questions?' etc. etc. I persisted however, and he told me he had met the girl in a place called The Rialto, a broken down old bridge. He had given her money and they had repaired to a nearby house, whereupon Roderick discovered the most Alarmg. Intelligence, viz: that the Powers of Venus had totally deserted him!

'I was as impotent as a babe,' he wailed, 'and not surprising either, after that d—d French Duke had shot at my balls from three feet range. I knew the shock would prove fatal.'

His Amatory Powers hvg. proved insufficient, Roderick demanded the return of his money from the wench. When she refused he snatched it from a table and ran off back to the inn.

I tried to console Roderick by pointg. out that the relaxation of his Nervous Fibres was undoubtedly due to the shock of hvg. a musket fired in such close proximity to the Vital Meckanism. Time must surely heal, since there was no injury, and we would have him treated by the finest Doctors meanwhile. After a while his gloom lifted and he cried, 'Damme if I don't try again tomorrow with another whore!'

Upon which we drank sevl. flasks of wine mixed with brandy and treacle to make it more palatable, and joined the Hon. C-F under the table.

*March 26*: Sleet. Signor Verdi turned green and died. Roderick rested throughout the day as he intended to make another trial of his Venusian Equippage in the eveng. In p.m. went to Opera to examine the highest Society.

Once more Dame Fortune favoured me. I had hardly

entered the Opera before a pair of Delicious
Protuberances presented themselves to my sight. Their
owner, one Signora Fulminazzione, found my addresses
by no means unwelcome and later I was allowed to
indulge in the Felicities of her Person at her house
before her husband returned home.

It was in a jovial mood I returned to the inn, and
celebrated by drinking a small barrel of wine. Alas, my
merriment was checked by the arrival of Roderick with
the sad news that once again the Amorous Faculty had
deserted him totally.

*March 27*: At breakfast a curious incident occurred,
viz: the bowl of the spoon dissolved in my chocolate. I
pushed it away untasted and a lackey drank it.
Immediately a jet of steam shot from his ears, his face
turned black and he expired with a shout of
'Fornicazione!'

I told the innkeeper my chocolate was poisoned. He
looked alarmed and said it was doubtless the work of
Signor Fulminazzione, the husband of my last night's
Conquest. 'If you have offended him,' he said, 'it would
be better to leave Venice. He will take any revenge where
honour is concerned.'

I stifled my fears as best I could and set out with the
Hon. C-F to view the city, whilst Roderick made another
trial of his Generative Machinery. I had hardly left the
inn before a knife whizzed past my face and stuck in the
door; an hour later a large stone was dropped upon me
from a high bldg. Thus we returned early to dinner, to
find Roderick in tears at yet another failure in the
Tournament of Venus.

*March 29*: This day called upon the British Consul to ask if he could recommend a doctor to treat Roderick. The Consul named a Physickan and then asked if I would like to see a copy of the *London Daily Register,* which I perused gladly. I had just read the Mortalities when my eyes fell on an item of such importance I could scarce believe it. This was as follows, viz:

We understand that yesterday a gentln., named Sir Josh. Foulacre, feelg. he had been insulted by some persons at a Ball at St. Marylebone challenged them all to a duel, notwithstandg. there were six persons involved. They met at dawn next morng., armed with swords. When they fell to, Sir Josh. immediately despatched three of his opponents, two more fled, and he shot the last. Havg. become master of the field he pursued those who had fled, but in doing so he tripped and his own pistol exploded. The ball passed through the heart and he expired immediately. He leaves a widow and daughter to mourn his passage.

Upon readg. these fateful words, I clasped The Consul by the hand and expostulated, 'Sir, you have made me the happiest man alive.' With which I hastened to find Roderick, who was broodg. over his troubles at the inn.

I told him now Sir Josh. was dead there was nothg. to prevent him returng. to England, and as for me, the fear of bailiffs was small beer compared with the certainty of death from which I was relieved. Further, I pointed out, there was now no obstacle to pressg. his suit with Sir Josh.'s wealthy daughter, Fanny. To which he replied, 'Only the loss of my Vital Powers' but I assured him that could be dealt with in England better than abroad.

We spent the day packg. our chest and hiring a diligence to take us on the first stage of the journey home tomorrow. In p.m. said farewell to the Hon. C-F with a sumptuous dinner; he will now travel to Rome.

*Here follows the customary gap in the Journal, as Haggard drank himself into a stupor - Ed.*

*April 19*: Rain. Being unable to obtain sufficient liquor, I this day regained consciousness in France.

As we sat down to dinner at our inn a person at the next table suddenly rose and emptied his soup over the waiter. Realisg. he must be English I introduced ourselves. He said he was a Mr. Gaddesby of Chiswick, a merchant travellg. to visit his agents in Europe. We soon became in animated conversation as the wine flowed and I suggested some harmless wagers. I wagered a guinea on Whom Could Put Out Their Tongue the Farthest (knowg. that Roderick's member is of inordinate length) but Mr. Gaddesby beat him by half-an-inch; this was followed by a wager on Waggling the Ears Speedily, but in vain as Mr. Gaddesby's vibrated like bees' wings.

I then wagered I could drink a bott. of wine quicker than he could. He beat me by four seconds. My spirits being quickened I wagered that I could eat and drink more than he could in the next hour and we set to.

*Editor's Note: It is inevitable that a gap should follow in the manuscript here. In fact, from internal evidence, it appears that Haggard did not write up his account of the mammoth eating and drinking contest until several days later as he was quite ill as the result of his rash wager. Fortunately, Roderick, although barely literate despite his University education (or perhaps because of it), kept a few scrappy notes, hardly fit to be dignified with the title Journal and these are appended.*

## Roderick's Journal

Father entered into a wayger with Mr. Gaddesby as to Hoom cd. Eat and Drinke Moast and lost after eatg. three chickens, five playtes of white tubes*, & 3 loaffs and drinkg. six botts of wyne. Mr. Gaddesby beet hymn by eatg. an extra plate of tubes and a tumblur of brandy: Father fell off his chair in a stewpor and cd. not be roused so next day we strapped hymn to the top of the coach and contd. the journey, he still being in a stewpor.

*Roderick's capacity as a a diarist lacked his father's vivid attention to detail: All we read next day is: 'Nothg. happened.' And the day after: 'Father awoak.' Then the Journal proper resumes – Ed.*

*April 23*: Mist. In a.m. recovd. my senses. Asked about Mr. Gaddesby and Roderick says that after I swooned one of his ears appeared to catch fire and he was put to bed. I have not been bested in a contest as To Whom Could Eat the Most for seven years, and then my opponent dropped dead next day.

*May 3*: This day arrived in Calais, the end of a tedious journey of which, thank God, I have known little. Spent p.m. searchg. for signs of the tunnel which the French are excavatg. under the Channel but they have concealed all traces of it with typical Gallic cunng. Tomorrow we take ship for England.

*Doubtless spaghetti or macaroni

# Chapter Eight
## The Return

*May 4*: Dover mortalities: Drowned, 3; shot by Excise men, 7; hanged for smuggling, 19. Crossed to Dover by the packet in a.m. A good wind, and the journey took only a few hours. Sentiments of the strongest nature animated my bosom as we trod upon our native soil again. My patriotism glowed. Upon landg. I could scarce refrain from kissg. the English soil but owg. to the turbulence of the voyage was obliged to vomit upon the sacred earth instead.

Spent the night at an inn. Ate a pease puddg. at supper, the first I have ate since settg. forth for the region of Garlick, Fricassees and Toads.

*May 5*: With what pleasure I gazed once more upon our native land as the coach carried us to London. My happiness was complete when we overtook a Scotchman walking along the turnpike, and Roderick assailed him with such comments as 'Ya, tell us what's up your kilt Jock,' and similar witticisms. Arrived late in London, assuming the identity of an Irish gentln., for fear of arrest. I thus informed the landlord Shamus O'Murphy and his son would be pleased to sample his hospitality.

*May 6*: Sleet. We have decided to stay at Oxford in Roderick's College while we find how affairs stand at home and perhaps borrow some money from his friend Willikins. Arrived in time for supper. Roderick's absence does not appear to have been remarked by his college, but that is not surprising, as the entire establishment spends its time drinkg. port and sleepg.

We were soon installed in Roderick's rooms, where we invited Willikins to join us, together with some more gay sparks. About midnight a porter arrived to complain that an empty bottle thrown from a window had struck the Bursar. Observg. the Bursar to be still standg. on the lawn below, I threw the servant at him and he was felled a second time, causg. much merriment.

When Willikins was almost incapable through drink, I broached the matter of a loan. He instantly complied.

'My dear Sir,' he said, pourg. some champagne into his ear by mistake, 'I am vastly obliged to anyone who has the kindness to allow me to do them a service. Pray state how much you require.'

I said 1,000£ would do for a start and dragged him to a table where I supported him and guided his hand to write out the draft, after which I let go of him and he fell to the floor where Roderick was already lyg. together with sevl. other students. Later I joined them, hvg. secured the precious draft in an inner pocket, and rejoiced that once again Fortune had smiled upon us in our hour of need.

*May 7*: Jeremiah Fishwick blown to pieces whilst tryg. to turn lead into gold. Upon risg. I took out the precious draft for 1,000£ and showed it to Roderick, who seemed little impressed.

'Are you not happy that we have such a large sum of money?' I exclaimed.

'Large sum of money be d—d' he replied. 'Have you not seen that the draft is signed by The Marquis of Granby?'

Upon percvg. this was indeed true, I threw a bucket of water over Willikins as he lay on the floor and sought an explanation. Willikins said it was no use, he might as well have signed the draft 'Frederick the Great' as in his own name, for his father has cut off his allowance and he is livg. by borrowg. from his Scout.

I endeavoured to restrain myself upon the receipt of this Intelligence, but was forced to relieve my feelgs. by throwg. a chamber pot out of the window at an elderly Don.

At noon a message arrived from the Warden invitg. me to dine with the Fellows. I accordingly attended. Before the meal the Chaplain arose and commenced to say some mumbo-jumbo in Latin, but I caused the Popish practice to cease with a well-aimed apple. I then tied a napkin round my neck and imitated the Chaplain v. wittily, viz: sayg. 'Hic, Haec, Hoc' sevl. times. As the Bursar failed to laugh I poured a jug of cream over his head. When the College port arrived I drank three decanters by myself without passg. it round. I then amused the company by throwg. fruit at various old portraits on the wall. After one particularly accurate discharge it was discovered I had aimed not at a picture but at the Warden himself, comg. through the door, and he was carried away, hvg. been struck upon the head by a pineapple.

Just when my animation was at its highest I was

suddenly lifted out of my chair by two strong college servants, and escorted to Roderick's rooms, where the servants assisted me to enter by throwg. me through the door. I found Roderick lyg. upon the floor with a large smile upon his countenance. His expression was so strange that I feared he had taken some poison.

I asked him what was the matter that he should look so, and he replied, 'Matter? Matter? I will tell you what is the matter, Father. I have just seen, spoken to, and made amends with Fanny Foulacre, that is all!'

*May 8*: Rain. Jas. Trump d. from Seethg. of the Bile. Midnight struck as Roderick made his announcement. I pressed him to explain further and he told me he had met Fanny in the High with her Aunt, whom she was visitg. She seemed delighted to see him and persuaded her Aunt to invite us both to tea today, sayg. archly she was sure he would have much to say to her.

Upon this news I seized Roderick fervently by the hand, and indeed almost kissed him in a transport of joy. I told him this was our greatest chance. With Sir Josh. removed it was yet possible for the weddg. to take place, as I had observed a not unfriendly look in the eye of the mother.

We arose early and Roderick spent the day groomg. himself for the visit to his Intended. In view of the importance of the occasion he took a Bath, although it was but six months since his previous immersion. In p.m. we attended at the house of Fanny's Aunt, near Magdalen Bridge. My expectations rose immediately we entered the room and Fanny coloured deliciously at the sight of Roderick. Her Mother and her Aunt were present as well, and I detected a certain warmth in the pressure of the Mother's hand. I expressed our deep sorrow at the death of Sir Josh.

'I regret we did not part from Sir Josh. on better terms,' I said, endeavourg. to make a tear start in my eye.

To my surprise Fanny burst out, 'You mean Father desired to kill you.'

Her Mother said 'Hush child,' without much conviction. The Aunt said, 'My brother was always a very violent person. I remember as a child his favourite occupation was killg. things. There was not a livg. creature within five miles of the house.' In short, I gathered Sir Josh.'s death was not regretted a great deal.

I ventured a question about the estate.

'Apart from a legacy to his sister Charlotte,' said the Mother, 'it was all left to me, there being no other relatives. Of course, Fanny has a legacy of 20,000£ and an annuity for life.' Upon hearg. this intelligence I could scarce control myself. I rapped Roderick smartly upon the shin with my shoe and mouthed, 'Take Fanny into the garden.'

She took the hint if he couldn't, and led him away, whilst the Aunt went upstairs. On being left alone with the Mother I told her that Roderick was still devoted to Fanny, notwithstandg. the Unpleasantness that occurred. I believed Fanny was not indifferent to Roderick: in short, would she agree to a match? She replied she had never agreed with her late husband's harsh judgement on either of us. She did not see why Roderick should have been blamed for the Impetuosity of Youth.

'Indeed sir,' she said, with a meang. glance at me, 'I understand only too well how difficult it is to resist the tender passions that rest in the bosom.'

'Madam,' I replied, 'you are too kind,' but got no

113

further before the d—d woman flung herself upon me and bore me to the ground in a passionate embrace. I was hard put to stop her indulging in the Delights of Venus there and then, which might have marred all had we been discovered. I gave her to understand that her passion should be gratified at the right moment. Roderick returned and I took him aside and told him there was no impediment to the match. He assured me Fanny was willing and after an exchange of mutual felicitations all round, we retired.

We celebrated with a sumptuous regale in College, but towards the end of the eveng., when Willikins and the other guests were amusg. themselves by wagering as To Whom Could Make the Others Vomit by Recallg. Unpleasant Things, my son grew pensive. I asked him why he did not join in his favourite game, which he would surely have won with his description of the Hunt Supper but he said he had no spirits. When pressed he confessed he was afraid his marriage to Fanny would be ruined through the Failure of The Amatory Parts.

I offered him money to test himself once more with one of the better class of whore, those frequented by Dons rather than the students, but he declined, sayg. he felt too low, even though I offered to pay for Merton Meg, the private whore maintained by that college.

*May 9*: Sevl. Fellows of Brasenose College today marked an anniversary by toastg. each other in Commemoration port. They continued for sevl. hours when the College Principal suddenly turned black, smoke came from his head and with a shout of 'Eheu Fugaces! O, Pallida Mors! Omnes eodem cogitur,' he expired to cries of, 'Well done, Principal, very apt, try using the subjunctive next time,' etc. etc.

*May 11*: This day we returned to Haggard Hall, the proud possessors of a draft for 1,000£ bestowed upon us by Fanny's Mother, who is now a wealthy woman. Thus armed, I could snap my fingers at the officers and others. I had sent money to my Lawyer to pay the worst debts, so our comg. was known and a large crowd greeted us on the turnpike. With many cheers they unyoked the horses and themselves dragged the carriage through the streets, only to swerve aside and dump the carriage in the pond, urged on by Blind Billy, who waved his stick and mouthed curses.

My wife Tib also greeted us with abuse, shoutg. 'Do you not know what I have had to bear what with the lawyers and the bailiffs' but I quieted her in the only way I know to silence a female, and that is by givg. her gold. Upon receipt of a bag of sovs. she became as silent as a tomb, if less useful and decorative.

*May 12*: How pleasant to return to familiar scenes and the ordered Domestick Routine of a country gentln. Evicted Snivelling Samuel in a.m. Walked the grounds inhalg. the delights of an English morn. The Human Heart could not but rejoice with news that the price of barley had risen by three-farthgs. a bushel. Saw the first swallow I have observed since returning from Europe, swoopg. merrily among the trees. Shot it.

Walked down High Street, the tradesmen fawning upon me, rubbg. their hands now they know I have money. My original intention was to horsewhip them but Nature was not strong enough for me to do so and I contented myself with salutations such as ramming their heads in their own wares, whereupon they bowed and invited me to assault their persons again.

Ate a giblet pie and a capon for dinner. Grunge havg. been paid, the capon's demise was comparatively recent.

*May 13*: Thunder. Mortalities: Reduction of The Fluid, 2: Removal of The Stone, 1. In addition Amos Nettlebed was jumping up and down on the grave of Thos. Cartwright (who died owg. him sixpence) when he slipped and fell and broke his skull and is not like to live.

In a.m. read old copies of *The Patriot* to acquaint myself with any executions etc. durg. my absence. Am v. worried about Roderick, who will not name the day of his weddg. in the hope a cure may be found before then for the failure of his Venusian Apparatus. Neither does he like to anticipate the Weddg. Rites, lest he should fail and Fanny call off the ceremony. Yet if the marriage miscarries all our hopes will fail.

'It is no use doing nothing,' I cried, 'we must seek a cure. Let us start with an Apothecary,' with which he reluctantly agreed.

*May 14*: Today visited the local Apothecary who is renowned for havg. cured Dismal Desmond of the Spasmodick Putrefactions with an extract made from toad's liver when all hope had been given up. On hearg. the facts he nodded wisely and said there was an infallible remedy in these cases, viz: an Aphrodisiacal Pie, made from the boiled testicles of a young bull.

Roderick turned pale at this and said he was d—d if he'd eat a bull's private parts for anyone; and in any case how could a man have a — after eatg. a mess like that? But I persuaded him and we took the receipt home where it was prepared for dinner.

Upon Roderick stickg. his fork in the pie a cloud of evil-smellg. vapour arose, and he started from the table, but I dragged him back and forced him to eat most of the dish. He then set out to call on Sordid Susan and test the efficacy of the cure.

But alas, he returned some hours later, sayg. that not only were the Vital Powers still lackg., but he had been sick as well.

*May 15*: Sleet. Amos Nettlebed died. His end was hastened by Thos. Cartwright's widow, who appeared at his window stickg. out her tongue and makg. vulgar signs at him as he lay sick and cryg. this would teach him to dance on honest folk's graves.

The weather has been unusually cold recently for the time of the year and walkg. down the High Street I was accosted by a mendicant asking for money to buy fuel for his family. I replied to him with the wittiest remark I have ever made in my life, which was as follows viz: 'If your family have no wood or coal, let them heat coke.'

The fellow was struck dumb by my sagacity, and made no reply.

*May 16*: Hail. Mortalities: the Lungs, 3; the Lumps, 4; the Lassitude, 5. The weather continues wet and cold. Five ailing lambs have been brought into the kitchen where Mrs. Runcible is tending them. She being at her wits end how to feed them, as there is no milk owing to an outbreak of cattle fever, I told her to give them port and brandy copiously.

*May 17*: Sleet. Obadiah Milestone d. for no apparent reason. He owed me three halfpence. The lambs continue to thrive on their unusual diet, which does not surprise me. I myself have lived largely upon the same regimen for forty years and apart from an occasional attack of Fowl Pest am as well as any man in the Kingdom.

In view of the weather indulged myself with a good dinner of some pig's face, boiled mutton, lungs, smelts, fritters and a raisin puddg. Found a piece of toenail in the puddg. Grunge says it could not be his as he was taught by his mother to bite his toenails to keep them short. He offered to demonstrate but I refused.

*May 18*: Sleet. Thos. Fogg died by his own hand. He had never been joyed since the price of oats rose and was further saddened by a fall in the value of stocks. Even the recent death of his wife failed to cheer him.

The Coroner has sat upon Obadiah Milestone and declared he died for no apparent reason. I called at his house to ask the widow for my halfpenny but she has already taken up with Well-Endowed William who would not let me in. Half-Witted Jack severely beaten by Short-Sighted Samuel who mistook him for a horse.

Disturbed after dinner by a terrible bleating sound like the Rector delivering a sermon and discovered to my horror that there were two hundred sheep gathered outside the hall peering in the direction of the kitchen. At that moment Mrs. Runcible burst into the room and said a vast number of sheep had forced their way into the kitchen and were consuming every drop of brandy and port within sight.

Scarce had she spoke when I saw a further flock of

five hundred approaching the hall from the direction of Lower Sodmire. I instantly cried out, 'They want the same diet as the lambs! Give them a pail of calomel instead and they will go away!' So she sped to the kitchen and suited action to the word, and within a few minutes nothing could be heard but the sound of sevl. hundred sheep retiring at high speed. ITEM: Bucket of calomel, 0£ 0s. 1½d.

N.B. One of the sheep was Half-Witted Jack in disguise.

*June 28*: Wm. Doorpost d. from the Spanish Eruptions. Enoch Oatmeal caught swine fever from sleepg. with the pigs while drunk. He often did this as his wife would not let him in the house. Latterly he said he preferred it. Returned home today, for the last month havg. been at Foulacre Hall with Fanny and Lady Foulacre. Visited Sir Josh.'s grave and made rude signs at it. The weddg. has been fixed for October, principally because Fanny comes into some more money if she reaches the age of thirty unwed. Poor Roderick would delay the weddg. until his Powers were restored but we cannot procrastinate any further; Fanny does not seem anxious to anticipate the Marriage Rites and Roderick dare not do so lest his Weakness be revealed.

Since the weddg. date has been agreed I felt we should make another attempt to cure Roderick. I therefore took him to Dr. Bone, who said he was suffering from a surfeit of blood which had caused a Relaxation of the Nervous Fibres and must be bled. He applied some leeches to Roderick's arm. At first these expired on tastg. his blood but sufficient survived for the purpose and Dr. Bone announced himself satisfied.

Roderick declared he felt much better for his bleedg. and wished to test its efficacy at once. I therefore returned to the Hall while he set out on foot for the establishment of a local harlot.

As I was sittg. down to dinner there was a knock at the door and Grunge came in to say two men had just delivered Roderick into the hall. I went outside and found him lying on the floor with a ghastly pallor on his face.

His breeches were torn and I asked if he had been attacked. He replied no, upon leavg. the doctor's house he had set out briskly for the harlotry but unfortunately the house was up a steep hill and loss of blood made the exertion of climbg. too much. Halfway there he was compelled to crawl.

'I got to the house exhausted,' said Roderick, 'and fell helpless on the doorstep for half an hour after which I'd just enough strength to knock on the door. I call it a knock though damme it was more like a gnat beatg. its foot. Eventually, the old b— who ran the place opened the door and I handed over my money and asked her to go inside and find me a sturdy girl. To my fury the d—d woman refused. 'If you can't cross the threshold without assistance you won't be much use inside,' she said.

'I attempted to raise myself but collapsed on the doorstep blockg. the door, so she went away and came back with a shovel and scraped me off like a dog's turd and then slammed the door.'

Roderick was put to bed with a bott. of port while I thought deeply about our dilemma.

*July 8*: Gales. The country has been struck by terrible winds. Josh. Wart was slain by a chimney pot which fell on him, although it did not fall from a roof but was wielded like a club by his wife. *The Patriot* says that in Kensington Village near London the wind blew a cow right over a barn along with the milkmaid and her bucket, yet neither suffered hurt and the girl continued milkg. as they sailed through the air. When a whore on Westminster Bridge lifted her skirt to oblige a Member of Parliament the wind got under it and blew her across the Thames to Southwark, where before she could compose her dress another gentln. offered her money.

*July 17*: Nathaniel Furnace d. from the Putrifying Spasms. Percvd. a great stir and sound of drums in The Square in a.m. and found a recruiting sergeant enlisting men for service in America. His name is Sergt. Kite and he has pasted up notices sayg. 'All lusty lads who have not enough ale and too much wife are to repair to the sign of The Crown where Sergt. Kite is now enlisting men in the 999th Foot ("The White Feathers") for service in America against the rebel Colonialists. Every man to receive a shillg. on enlistment and five guineas on joining the regiment. N.B. When in the field, every man to receive a halfpenny a day in lieu of food.'

A great throng pressed round the Sergeant. Blind Billy and Limping Leonard tried to enlist, seekg. money, free food and liquor. Their ruse might have succeeded as Billy supported Leonard, who guided him, but when Billy took his arm away to scratch himself Leonard fell over and Billy walked into a wall and raised his hat to it. Sordid Susan, one of the whores, tried to enlist disguised as a man, but as she was suckling a babe her Stratagem was discovered.

The Sergeant's enthusiasm knew no bounds, however, and every able-bodied man foolish enough to come within twenty yards was in danger of being enlisted, includg. the Rector, who, seeg. the Sergeant had a pile of money in front of him, innocently asked, 'Could you give me change for a half-a-guinea, my good fellow?'

'Certainly your honour,' replied the Sergeant, and handed him ten shillings and sixpence.

As the Rector was thankg. him he suddenly shouted, 'You hv. taken the King's Shillg.! You are enlisted!' With which he called two of his men who dragged him away and he was only released when he bribed the Sergeant.

*July 18*: At breakfast Grunge announced he was joining the army. 'I have spoken to Sergt. Kite,' he said, 'and he assured me I would not only get threepence a day regular, but also free drink and vittels, includg. a pound of beef and a pound of bread, which is better than I fare here.'

I tried hard to dissuade him. 'Grunge!' I ejaculated, 'you may not be paid regularly but you are not actually shot at, or at least, not more than two or three times a year.' Alas, the poor fool would not be moved and went to see Sergt. Kite. Some hours later there was terrible commotion outside and Grunge banged on the door shoutg. 'Hide me sir!' He told me that when he went to the Sergeant he asked him to wait while he flogged a man who had enlisted and then tried to run away. At this Grunge himself fled and now feared he would be pursued and flogged.

So for a few hours he hid in the cellar and when he

ventured forth, fear made him the perfect servant. But later, when he realised the Sergeant was not pursuing him he soon relapsed into his usual insolent self, so that I wished the Sergeant had taken him.

# *Chapter Nine*
## *The Knot is Tied*

*July 21*: Drought. No rain has fallen for some weeks; everywhere is parched and brown. Water is in such short supply, the girls at Lower Sodmire insist upon being paid with a jug of water, yet there are still no takers. The wells are dry and the streams dried up. Old Mother Gumboil, who is believed to be a witch, says a way of curing thirst for good is to drink the bile of a dead horse, but nobody dares try. The Rector, however, believes the drought is a punishment for a Great Sin committed in the Parish.

Spent a.m. broodg. as to who might have committed the Great Sin and gave my list to the Rector. There was Silas Brown, who demanded higher wages; Seth. Sidewinder, who is suspected of having married his aunt; Bart. Kettle, who sold me a sick sheep and the maid at The Crown, who refused to let me look at her delicious bubbies even though I offered her a farthg.

The Rector says he fears the sin is more grievous; perhaps Fornication, Debauchery, or even Blasphemy. at which he looked me in the eye pointedly.

*July 22*: Drought. Old Mother Gumboil says rain will come if everybody eats the raw liver of a newly-dead rat. Josh. Burp got drunk and dived into the old quarry for a swim but alas it had dried out, and he died instantly, since it is 60 feet deep.

For my shavg. water this morning I was forced to lather my cheeks in a bottle of Château Yquem which I had bought to celebrate the victory of Genl. Burgoyne over the American Rebels under the traitor Washington. Alas, it will never be needed.

The Rector offered prayers for rain today and blamed the drought on 'A Great Fornicator in the parish' at which I muttered 'Great Fiddlesticks' and then pretended to snore. Wise Grandpa Hayfork, the parish sage, said in The Crown tonight that a drought always ends when the sparrows fly towards the sun in the evening; or perhaps it was the morning, he could not remember which. Later he said it was not sparrows but thrushes and it wasn't the sun but the moon. A little later they carried him out.

Ate some pigeons, a leg of mutton, and a piece of cow's udder for dinner. Cleansed the teeth in Bollinger.

*July 24*: Drought. Percvg. a large throng in The Square in a.m. I found Old Mother Gumboil declarg. she would create rain by drinking the blood of a snake in front of everybody, which she then did. She died immediately. Wise Grandpa Hayfork says it is a sure sign that wet weather is coming when the voles stand on their hind legs and dance vertically round in circles, holdg. each other's paws. He says there is an old sayg. in the district:

> When voles in circles go
> Wet weather sure to blow.

Eph. Smith said he had it wrong, it was 'dry weather sure to blow', and it was not voles but stoats. They fell on each other and had to be dragged apart.

In p.m. to the funeral of Josh. Burp. The coffin was square, this now being his own shape owing to fallg. from such a great height. Just as they were about to lower the coffin into the grave water was percvd. trickling into it from out of the earth and within a few moments the trench was flooded to a depth of three feet.

The coffin was hastily hauled out and thrown to one side whilst everybody ran to fill jugs and jars with the precious fluid. As for me, I commanded Grunge to fetch two buckets, which he havg. filled, I told him to take one back to the hall whilst I took the other straight to Perverted Polly, at Lower Sodmire, who was by now offerg. special services for as little as a cupful and since my bucket contained at least a gallon I looked forward to bathg. for a long time in the Waters of Aphrodite.

*July 31*: Rain. Bart Thistle d. from the Peripneumony but when the Coroner sat on him he declared an open verdict as he could not spell it. Roderick and I journeyed to Oxford today havg. heard a learned Fellow in the Natural Sciences was using the newly-discovered Electrick Fluid for cures for divers diseases and there was hope he might aid Roderick's Condition.

*Aug. 1*: Met learned Fellow at Lincoln College and he told me the discovery of the Electrick Fluid opened new possibilities. 'It is being tried as a treatment for Insanity, Pox, Gout, Ague, The Spasms and many other diseases,' he said.

I asked if it was successful, to which he replied, 'Half the patients fully recovered.'

'And the other half?'

'They died.'

My knowledge of the Fluid being scanty I assumed Roderick would merely have to annoint himself or drink A Potion so I assented. Was astonished when the Fellow led us into a room in a Spital with an audience of some score of doctors etc. Before I could protest Roderick was strapped to a table and his breeches removed. I was about to intervene when the Fellow assured me there would be no surgery. He showed me two wires attached to a glass jar between felt pads, which he called a Leyden Jar. The wires were attached to Roderick's Parts, and the jar rapidly revolved by a handle.

The awful sight which followed will remain long in my memory. As the jar revolved there was a great crackling sound and sparks shot from Roderick's Loins. At the same time he gave a fearful cry, raised himself half-upright, and sank back with a moan.

I demanded his release but the Fellow assured me there was no cause for alarm; the cure lay in the shock occasioned by the Electrick Fluid. Indeed he thought a second administration might prove valuable.

Roderick, however, would have none of it and was helped from the buildg. bent double. ITEM: To the Electrick Fluid 2£ 1s. 9¹/₂d.

*Aug. 2*: Gave Roderick a shillg. to find a woman; a good-class girl such as the Provost might use. He returned complaining. the Amatory Organs were totally numbed by the Electrick Shock. 'D— it' he complained, 'they've no sensation at all. It felt like the time I fell through the ice at Christmas and then it took two hours before I could hold a glass of brandy, let alone a wench.'

After this I decided to have no more Quack Nostrums but to await the healg. effect of time. The weddg. must take place as arranged.

*Aug. 10*: Rain. Obadiah Horn d. from the Windy Spasms. While I stood in the Square the Constable approached and warned me that grave disorders were expected this week with the Great Knurdling Match in two days' time. The Knurdling is an ancient contest between Upper and Lower Sodmire which is played with a Knurdle or small wooden ball, which both sides have to propel with their noses through the streets. Upper Sodmire hv. to reach Lower Sodmire Parish Church and Lower Sodmire must drive the Knurdle to the Market Cross at Upper Sodmire.

*Aug. 11*: Hail. In view of the Constable's warning I visited the village today to swear in some more constables to maintain order but the only men we could find were Blind Billy, Crippled John, Palsied Peter, Half-Witted Jack and Lame Bob, all the able-bodied men hvg. kept out of the way. Nevertheless I swore them in, hoping the rioters will waste time jumping up and down on Palsied Peter, which will gain a respite for me to reach safety.

Recvd. from Wm. Burdock the sum of 0£, 0s. 3½d. for a sheep, which he paid cheerfully, not knowing the sheep was diseased, being infected with The Wobbles.

*Aug. 12*: To Stretchford in p.m. for The Great Knurdle. There was a vast crowd to watch the proceedings, most already far gone in liquor. At first our men pushed the Lower Sodmire men back as far as the Parish pump, but the match soon swung the other way because of the strength of the Lower Sodmire team's noses, which they prepare by rubbing the organ with linseed oil twice a day.

Eventually Lower Sodmire reached the pound and were declared the winners, receiving 10 sovs., a firkin of ale and a giblet pie, after which their supporters began to celebrate by breaking all the windows in the High Street.

I tried to divert them to the property of my enemies, crying, 'Hey there, you brave lads, why not break open this house, the owner is a canting Lawyer,' etc. etc. but they paid no attention, as Wm. Burdock was privily pointing out houses belonging to myself, which in time they broke into, using Lame Bob as a human battering ram, due to the unusual flatness of the top of his head.

Thus I returned home sore and weary and ate a leg of mutton for supper. After I had eaten it Grunge informed me he bought it cheap off Wm. Burdock and I realised it was the diseased sheep I sold him. ITEM: Emeticks, $0£$ 0s. $0^1/_2$d.

*Aug. 16*: Rain. Thos. Haddock died from the Howling Spasms. Evicted Sturdy Thomas for forming a Combination among the labourers.

*Aug. 20*: Mist. Jas. Chilblain died from The Splenetick Convulsions as he sat down to dinner. His wife, being of a thrifty nature, finished her meal and then ate his as well before calling the doctors.

*Aug. 30*: Roderick returned home today, hvg. spent some time at Foulacre Hall, with his beloved Fanny and her mother. I could not bring myself to mention the Delicate Subject of his Amatory Machinery, upon which so much depends, but pointed at his breeches and raised my eyebrows; at which he shook his head sadly. Later he told me he dare not test the Meckanism with Fanny, but made a trial with a whore recommended by the butler at Foulacre Hall. Not only did he fail, but discovered the wench was the butler's sister.

*Sept. 2*: Storms. Mortalities: Because Their Time Had Come, 1.

Arrived this day at Gibbet Hall, seat of Sir Humph. Frogworthy, for a few days' shootg. Roderick came with me, as I thought it might take the boy's mind off his troubles. Also Grunge.

Sir Humph. treated the guests to a grand regale in the p.m. but such was the strength of my potations that I can only remember the first remove, which contained some tongues of exceptional size, which caused me to utter one of the most risible remarks of my life, viz: 'By the size of the tongue, it must have been a female animal.'

None laughed louder at this mirthful sally than Lady Humph., a woman of Indeterminate age and hideous complexion, but one to whom Nature had been generous in the allocation of those Protuberances which so easily excite the male passions. Sensing my dilemma, Roderick nudged me and animadverted, 'When puttg.

more coal on the fire one does not examine the mantelpiece, father,' and the decision was made for me after dinner when the lady invited me to look at the family portraits upstairs.

Within two minutes we were worshipping at The Temple of Venus in her bedroom when I heard the sound of running feet. Knowg. Sir Humph. to be a jealous husband I gathered up a basin of water and as he opened the door flung it over his wife with a cry of 'Fire! Fire! I was only just in time!'

*Sept. 3*: Drizzle. Eph. Harbottle d. of the Spasmodick Rumblings. Am not sure Sir Humph. was deceived by my strategem; he gave me a strange look at breakfast. Then to the shootg. where I had immediate success, spottg. a bird which suddenly appeared in my sights only a few feet to one side of me. I let fly with my fowlg.-piece and it crashed down immediately.

I was capering with delight when a gentln. whom I remembered from last night approached and shouted 'D— you sir, you did not hit a bird; you have shot off my hat.' On closer inspection I percvd. I had indeed shot his hat, which looked remarkably like a bird.

'Sir, if you choose to dress in a hat like a partridge you must not blame me if I shoot it,' I replied with dignity. Unfortunately, that was the only success I achieved in a.m., as it took Grunge so long to reload and twice he put the bullets in before the gunpowder. Eventually I used him as a retriever and he was much more useful, excelling all the other dogs in bringing back birds in his mouth.

At midday a vast cold collation was presented with sevl. vats of cold punch after which the sport waxed even more fast and furious. Sevl. times I discharged at what turned out to be spots in front of the eyes while one gentln. claimed to have peppered a pink elephant. The final bag was as follows, viz: 951 brace of partridge; seventeen windows; a chimney; three cattle; two keepers; five poachers and three guests.

*Sept. 4*: Rain. After our exertions of yesterday it was a disappointment to find all able-bodied birds had fled, leavg. behind only a few too weak to get away. Furthermore, all animal and bird life had departed the neighbourhood, together with most of the human inhabitants.

As we stood surveying the silent desolation, and wondering what to do, Sir Humph., who had an angry look in his eye, addressed the party. 'Gentln.,' he said, 'it is obvious we must have poor sport today unless some substitute for the birds is found,' to which we all cried 'Hear, hear .'

'Therefore,' he continued, 'I have a suggestion to make. Let us seek a new target for our guns, one that will provide healthy sport before it is finally brought crashing down by our combined fire.'

'And what do you suggest as our new target?' I cried.

'You, sir!' he said fiercely. 'A damned adulterer that would debauch his host's wife in his own home. You are fittg. game sir, and the sport will commence as soon as we can load!'

With which I waited no more but with animation that surprised me fled into the distance pursued by the sound of gunfire from thirty barrels. ITEM: Bandages and Plaisters: 0£ 6s. 8d.

*Sept. 9*: Rain. Evicted Caleb Golightly because I did not like him. D——d dull. Hv. not spat on half-a-dozen persons all week. Roderick is stayg. with friends; haply it may cure the gloom with which he views his approachg. nuptials.

*Sept. 12*: Fog. Knowg. I am like to have money soon, the Rector called and said he had not recvd. any Tithes for five years. Further, the Great Tithe Barn was completely empty and now only used by the labourers to relieve themselves in (which is true, as the outside jakes collapsed recently). I told him I would consider the matter.

*Sept 13*: Thunder. Dumped half a ton of manure outside the Rectory front door with a note on it sayg. 'Tithe'.

*Sept. 14*: The Rector came to complain about the manure. I apologised that it was only one year's tithe, but if he wished I would dump another four years' worth tomorrow. At which he went away.

*Sept. 15*: Rain. Samuel Foghorn died from The Stinking Exhalations.

*Sept. 20*: Floods. The wet weather has affected my health and I am plagued by pains in the joints, so severe I can hardly walk. Tried to visit the grounds but was jeered at by sevl. poachers who knew I could not pursue them. Called Dr. Bone and he commanded me to take a freshly-caught trout and a raw onion and tie them to my knee with a bandage and sit with my feet in a bowl of rhubarb water.

*Sept. 22*: Rain. I continue ill and unable to move. The cure has done no good and the trout tied to my knee has gone bad and smells. Confined to my bed I thought longingly about the joys of spring and its flowers and penned the following lines:

> For oft, when on my couch I lie
> In vacant or in pensive mood
> They flash upon that inward eye
> Which is the bliss of solitude;
> And then my heart with pleasure fills,
> And dances with the daffodils.

Grunge said it was very good and asked permission to copy it for a friend who was interested in poetry.

In p.m. I was consoling my sick body with some smelts, baked hearts, a pease puddg. and five or six botts. of Madeira when Grunge suggested a cure his grandmother had used, viz: to mix up a potion of ground frogs' eyes, beetles' blood and spiders' heads and drink it while facing North.

'Did she recover?' I asked and he replied, 'Yes, within twelve hours she was fully restored to her normal vigour, nay, she was better than before.' I was about to order him to collect some of this elixir when he added, 'She dropped dead two days later. We have never been able to understand why.' My wife Tib says her mother used to treat her father with a piece of dung tied to the affected parts. I animadverted, 'Ha, ha, that mayhap accounts for why he had no friends,' but she flounced out, the jest being too subtle for her.

*Sept. 23*: Storms. As I sat thinking a plague upon these pesky cures, I found myself looking at a portrait of Sir Percy Haggard, who fought on both sides in the Civil War and who was supposed to hv. eaten a spoonful of gunpowder every day, claiming it a sure cure for every ill. Collecting some from the gunroom I poured it into my port and drank the lot.

Two hours later the rheumatism had vanished and I felt perfectly well apart from a slight buzzing in the head. I danced like a child and calling for Grunge told him the good news. But he only stared and ejaculated, 'Sir, have you not noticed your face?'

Looking in the mirror I discovered to my dismay that my face was covered in huge purple warts and an examination of Sir Percy's picture revealed that he, too, was covered in similar warts which I had believed to be blemishes on the canvas. ITEM: Emeticks: 0£ 0s. 0½d.

*Sept. 24*: Rain. Recvd. from Thos. Welkin one farthg., which his father owed me before he died last harvest. To the village in a.m. to evict Granny Dormouse but she was out, so I contented myself with makg. faces at her cat, which fled precipitately.

Hearing a snivelling noise behind me in the street I percvd. the Rector, who asked if he could use my barn for a Harvest Supper for the Deserving Poor. I asked whom the guests would be and he replied he intended to invite Blind Billy, Palsied Peter, Granny Dormouse, Goody Bramble, Little William the chimney sweep's boy, and many others.

At this my brow grew black. 'You have just named the biggest scoundrels in the parish!' I ejaculated. 'Know you not Blind Billy voted against the Tory candidate at the last election? As this is a Rotten Borough, the Whig was elected by two votes to one. As for the others, they are all behind with their rents, except Little William and the Christmas before last he spoiled our festivities by getting stuck in the chimney for three days, so we were unable to light a fire and had to have a cold dinner. Yet he did nothg. but whine and howl the whole time with no thought of the trouble he was causg. He would be there yet if I had not blown him out with gunpowder.'

With which I bade the cringing Clerick trouble me no more as I would hold my own dinner for those who were truly deservg. But the Rector insisted on attending, as he said he might do some good among the unhappy creatures I would invite.

*Sept. 25*: Sleet. Wm. Trumpet hanged himself because nobody liked him. Spent a.m. planning my dinner. Instead of the idle, profligate paupers proposed by the Rector, I have decided to invite the most noble, abused and deservg. people I know, namely the local whores.

Sent Grunge out to deliver invitations, and he returned sayg. all had accepted except Sordid Susan, of Lower Sodmire, who would be busy at the Mayor's Banquet. Also absent would be Ferocious Fanny, who had tragically died in strange circumstances. Plying her trade with a sentry at the barracks, she placed his musket against the wall while they conjoined in those Ceremonies sacred to Aphrodite. Alas, such was the animation of their Conjunction, the vibration caused the musket to slide to the ground, where it exploded, and the ball passed through both, killg. them instantly.

*Sept. 28*: Drizzle. Bart. Bugle died from the King's Evil. In p.m. to my dinner in the barn where some thirty poor souls congregated. When the meal was well advanced I proposed a Toast to all present, in these words: 'Let us remember at this time,' I said, 'that they who humbly toil in the bagnio or the bedchamber or behind the churchyard wall, serve mankind as well as those who sit on a royal throne. Let him that is perfect cast the first stone.'

My speech was greeted with thunderous applause and Unclean Ursula rose to reply as follows, viz: 'I ain't much good at speaking, —ing's more in my line.' (Loud cheers and cries of agreement, followed by collapse of sevl. whores.) 'But I'll tell you this – the Squire's as true an English gentln. as ever gave threepence to a poor girl who pleasured him, and if he wants it for twopence, then he can come to Ursula any time!' which generous oration was recvd. with further applause.

Alas, as the wine flowed, human nature proved too strong for the good ladies, and they could not resist plying their trade. Lewd Lorna began lifting her skirt and winking at the Rector while Perverted Polly, with a hideous leer, pressed herself against him, causing the miserable Clerick to flee from the barn crying, 'Woe is me! Here is Babylon The Mother of Harlots and Abominations of the Earth, Revelations chapter eight, verse five.'

After which we made merry the whole night long. ITEM: To Unclean Ursula, 0£ 0s. 2d.

*Oct.1*: Drizzle. Jas. Spudwell died from The Exploding Palpitations. He owed me sixpence. This morning an earthquake occurred. On awaking I sat up to throw away a bottle of port I was clutching when to my astonishment the whole room started to vibrate and reel round. The tremor must have released some animals from a menagerie, because a crocodile was standing in the corner. It was some time before the earthquake ceased, yet nobody else in the house experienced it. Such are the Mysteries of Nature.

*Oct. 2*: Rain. This day Roderick, myself and Tib left the Hall for the seat of the Foulacres where we shall stay until the weddg. The villagers lined up as we passed along the main street and doffed their hats. This, however, proved to be not a token of respect as they had privily secreted pieces of dung in their headgear, which they hurled with abandon at the carriage. Half-Witted Jack threw a particularly large piece.

Arrived in p.m. to a warm welcome, v. different from our last visit. At supper Lady Foulacre remarked, 'You may drink as much as you please now, Mr. Haggard. We no longer have any restriction in that direction.' Remarkg. a purple hue in my Lady's complexion, which doubtless denoted a frequent resort to the cordial bottles, I took her at her word and knew no more until dawn, when I awoke behind the window curtain.

*Oct. 3*: Sun. Roderick is to be married tomorrow. In order to spare myself the discomfort of early risg. for the occasion, I decided to sit up all night with a few botts. of port. Roderick desired to join me but I forbade it, sayg. he would need all his strength for the morrow. Fanny's mother bade me goodnight with every token of the deepest affection, so far forgettg. herself as to wink and gesture with her thumb towards her bedroom, but I

have already told her we must not enlist in the ranks of
Venus's Battalion until after the marriage, as I fear my
wife will do us some dreadful hurt.

*Oct. 4*: Rain. About three in the a.m. I fell to broodg.
over Roderick's Weakness of the Loins, and what might
be done about it, and after much cogitation came to the
followg. conclusion viz: That as the original relaxation
of the Nervous Fibres was caused by the proximate
discharge of a musket, a cure might possibly be effected
by causg. a similar (although harmless) discharge to
take place near to Roderick, and the subsequent shock
might regenerate the Affected Parts. I therefore decided
to take action this eveng. although the explosion must
come as a surprise to Roderick if it is to be effective.

At ten o'clock a.m. we set off for church. Wondered
not for the first time what mysterious attraction drew
Fanny to my son, whom has nothg. about his person to
recommend him except the extraordinary elasticity of
his features, which enables him to win wagers as To
Whom Can Pull the Ugliest Face. The bride's Mother
had been partakg. of the Cordials freely, and was with
some difficulty guided to her right place in the sacred
edifice.

Words cannot express my joy as the parson
pronounced the couple man and wife. I joined him
loudly in sayg., 'Whom God hath joined together let no
man put asunder,' especially with a dowry like that.
Such was my elation when the couple were firmly
joined that as we gathered outside I privily spat upon
Sir Josh.'s grave, only to find that sevl. other persons
had done the same, whilst one had placed thereon a
posey of Deadly Nightshade.

The reception at the Hall had scarce begun when the door was flung open and a familiar voice cried, 'Haw, haw, haw, but damme I'm deuced glad that I got here in time,' and the figure of the Hon. Cholmondley-Fitzroy appeared. He had read about the weddg. in *The Gentlemen's Magazine* and posted here immediately from his family home in Sussex. He told us he had to leave Italy shortly after our departure, hvg. had the misfortune to seduce the mistress of the Duke of Milan, and he returned home for fear of his life as the Duke was a noted poisoner of any rival.

At length eveng. drew on, and Roderick and Fanny departed for the bridal chamber with many winks and bawdy jests which fell hollowly upon the ear of poor Roderick, who looked pale and drawn.

I took him aside and said, 'Do not despair. I have a Stratagem to make all well,' to which he replied, 'D— your Stratagem, Father, the only Stratagem that would help me would be a splint.'

Notwithstandg., I told him to come to the window of his chamber and wave a white handkerchief if the Amorous Powers failed him, and to leave the window open.

When the bridal couple had departed I stole into the garden and stationed myself where I might see their room, takg. with me my blunderbuss, which I had double charged with powder, omittg. the bullets. Their candle went out and still I waited, until after a quarter of an hour I percvd. a movement at the window, and a white handkerchief was waved forlornly behind the glass. I waited a few moments and then stole to the wall of the house and raised a ladder I had previously concealed there. Placg. this under Roderick's windowsill I climbed up, thrust my blunderbuss through the open window of the bridal chamber and fired it in the direction of the bed. The blast was like a clap of thunder in the confined space. Such was the intensity of the discharge that I was thrown backwards off the ladder, the window shattered in a thousand fragments, and I fell heavily to the earth below, where I struck my head and was knocked insensible.

I regained consciousness a little while later, and lookg. at my watch percvd. I had lain there for 10 minutes. Fearg. I had perhaps injured someone with my blast I was about to erect the ladder again when Roderick thrust his head through the shattered window and shouted, 'Father – are you there, Father? Father, the Amorous Powers are totally restored!' With which he began caperg. like a madman, cryg. out, 'I've got back me prowess! Damme, but I am totally restored to my Manly Vigour! The Parts are functioning like a New-comen Steam Engine!'

I called to him, 'Be quiet! We do not want the whole neighbourhood to know that you once lost your Generative Ability' and ran inside the house and up to his room. Fanny was in bed, blushg. sweetly whilst Roderick continued to caper about the chamber. Not trustg. Roderick to give a proper explanation, I told Fanny what had happened, stressg. heavily the shock occasioned to the Nervous Fibres by the discharge of the Frenchman's musket.

Alas, Roderick nearly spoiled all by askg. me for a shillg. for a whore, but at last I got him to understand he was married to the lady in the bed, and was not supposed to dress and leave the room halfway through the night.

So I left the happy pair with a father's benison and returned downstairs to drink myself into a stupor, in the firm belief that at last all our troubles were over. ITEM: To Purgatives, Emeticks and Physick, 0£ 0s. 0½d.